A BIT OF A CHALLENGE

For my wife Olive - for her love, friendship, support and help, which without I could never have achieved my ambition.

Acknowledgements

A big thank you to those who have helped me over the years through their friendship, talent and for just 'being there' including Michael Coveney, Nigel Brackley, Bob Tenninger, Barry Baker, Peter Wales, John Wallington, Kay Matthies, Joop Van Lent, Wil Snitjer, Deiter Schluter, Mark Kloska, Paul Pastecchi, Harald Reiter, Chuck Aaeron, all the people at Red Bull Hanger 8 Salzburg, Georg Maier and Bernd Bremer at Heli-Factory Germany, Simon Young, Curtis Youngblood, Wayne Mann, Cliff Hiatt, Hiro Hashimoto, David Sweatt, Darius Engineer, Peter Jakadofsky, Terry Hobday, Malcolm Watson, Andy Knightley, Kevin Casey, Matt Reuben, Peter Robinson and to the many other people whose names escape me at the moment.

Published in March 2011
Reprinted October 2011

A catalogue record for this book is available from the British Library.

ISBN 978-0-9568209-0-7

Published by STW Signs Ltd
70 Cerne Road
Gravesend,
Kent DA12 4BP

A BIT OF A CHALLENGE

US AMA Champion - for the fourth year running - 2009

LEN MOUNT
MICHAEL COVENEY

The life and times of a pioneer in the world of radio control helicopters

Right: Olive works on the assembly line.

Below: Just some of Len's trophies

CONTENTS

Preface

I have had a great career in doing something I love – building and flying radio control helicopters. When I first started there were no kits, in fact no one at that time even knew it was possible. It was only when someone challenged me to build one that I became engrossed in doing something that was a little different.

The challenges were huge – there were no such things as ball links or helicopter radios, there were no gyroscopes and the only engines you could get needed to be in a constant high-volume airflow from a propeller. Full-size helicopters are complex both mechanically and to fly. To do this in miniature was the holy grail of modelling throughout the 1960's and early 70's.

But I overcame them and soon became one of the early pioneers who had done the impossible. However, the challenges kept coming – inverted flying, performing aerobatics, installing jet engines – and as the sport grew I found myself competing and winning at a world-class level.

This wonderful hobby soon became my livelihood and I was launched into the world of TV and films, as well as taking part in strange engagements in Eastern Europe and the Arctic. I have flown in front of royalty, taught celebrities to fly and gained world records - not bad for someone who was considered to be uneducated and with no prospects.

The first part of this book contains reminisces of my long career while the second part focuses on how I approach building a world-class, scale radio-controlled model helicopter.

Whether you are a seasoned modeller, a weekend model pilot, or someone who is just fascinated by radio control helicopters, there should be something for you within these pages.

I do hope you enjoy the book and have as much fun in this great hobby, as I've had, and plan to continue doing so for a long time to come.

Len Mount

March 2011

www.lenmountscalehelicopters.co.uk

Introduction

I first met Len and his wife Olive in the summer of 2005, but I had known about him for at least 20 years prior to that.

In my teenage years I had been fascinated by radio control models – first with aeroplanes and then with cars. In those days to control an object remotely was a magical experience, even if those observing my efforts would not have used the word 'control'. The problem with aeroplanes is that crashing can be expensive and in my case always inevitable. Cars, on the other hand, while lessening the cost of the hobby, were not so exciting.

Then in the late 1970s and early 1980s things became more interesting as a few hardy pioneers demonstrated that it was possible to build and fly model helicopters. Up until this time, model helicopter flight was thought impossible due to the complexity of the mechanics, the heavy weight and hence large engine that would be required to power such a machine, and the sophisticated radio requirements necessary to control the wide range of inter-related moving surfaces. But these people were un-deterred and soon the problems had been solved and kits became available.

To my uneducated mind, here was something that could be flown slowly and therefore not prone to crashing as an aeroplane, and yet could be flown in the smallest of yards. Of course this perception was completely wrong but it didn't stop me dreaming of being able to fly from my own back garden.

But after buying my first kit – a Hirobo Shuttle - it became apparent that flying a model helicopter was not only difficult but also very expensive! Even building the model was hard. Whereas an aeroplane is quite easy to build or modify with the application of a sharp knife or superglue, this wasn't the case with a helicopter where it seemed you needed a degree in mechanical engineering and a lathe or similar large pieces of equipment.

And then there was setting them up. With an aeroplane about the only thing you need to adjust was the Centre of Gravity and the movement on a couple of wing surfaces. This could be checked by performing a gentle test glide, which if wrong would only result in a gentle, non-damaging bump. But with a helicopter there are around 10 times as many adjustments along with mastering the complexities of an on-board gyro, any one of which if setup wrong will cause the machine to self destruct and take out any person or object within a 20 metre radius.

Into this scene there appeared, to me anyway, a few 'gods' who made it all seem so simple. Not only could these people perform the most astounding aerobatic manoeuvres but they also did it by building models that actually looked like 'real' helicopters.

One such person was Len Mount. Len was (and still is at the time of writing) a 'giant' in the model helicopter world. He was one of the first (if not the first) person in the UK to build a flying model, a feat that took him 'just' a couple of years. He was also the first person to fly them inverted (an extremely difficult manoeuvre) and the first to fly a scale model powered by a miniature gas turbine engine.

After a while, my interest in the hobby waned due to time pressure from work and other interests. I sold my models and gave up the radio control helicopter scene, or so I thought. In the summer of 2005 I was organising my church's entry for a local carnival. We wanted to build a float that was different, something that would make people go 'wow'.

The initial design was to portray the old story of Jonah and the Whale. To make it interesting we installed several water pistols inside the whale's mouth so that it 'spat' at the crowd. This would certainly get us noticed but to my mind, this still wasn't enough to make people go 'wow'. We needed something else. At times like these my mind goes wild and I started to imagine what it would be like if the Jonah story happened today – surely they would send out a rescue helicopter to find him. And so the seed was sown. I imagined a scene where Jonah was in a tug-of-war between being swallowed by a whale and being rescued by a coastguard Sea King. But where could I get a helicopter?

My mind started going through all the people I had met in the past who could help out by providing a model helicopter. I had thought of making one but as we only had about 1 week before the carnival I had left it far too late. I then remembered one of my heros – Len Mount. I had never spoken to Len (although I had brushed past him at a model show in the 1980s) but I knew he lived in my locality. As I was desperate I typed his name into the search engine 'Google' and found his web site. I sent off an email asking if he could help and to my surprise he replied.

We then spoke on the phone and he said that I could hire one of his models (at the time he didn't know why I wanted to borrow it) for £200 and that I would have to pay him £3,000 if it was damaged while in my care. I hastily organised insurance cover and arranged to have the model delivered on the day of the carnival.

And so I met Len for the first time one Saturday morning in July 2005 as he handed over the machine - a beautiful scale Lynx that measured over two metres long. Unloading the model from his van was Olive, Len's quiet but supportive wife, who then helped to hang the model from the roof of the float. It was at this point I realised we had a small problem. Rather than the helicopter being representative of a coastguard search and rescue unit, it was a military machine complete with guns and rockets. So with a quick change of plan we decided to mount the helicopter so that it appeared to be attacking the whale. To add effect, Len suspended two rockets that appeared to have been launched from the helicopter.

As I looked at the completed scene, it was pretty obvious that this was no ordinary float – particularly one from a church. And that's the reaction we got from the crowd as the carnival procession worked its way through the town.

Everyone seemed to be pointing and staring at our float depicting the scene from some crazed American action film that could have been called 'Jonah meets Apocalypse Now'. Although not in keeping with the exact tradition of the Bible story, it certainly wowed the crowd as well as the judges as we were awarded 2nd prize.

When Len collected the model that evening I was so grateful to Len for entrusting strangers with one of his valuable creations. His models take many months to build and no amount of compensation could adequately replace this masterpiece. It was well worth the money. But to my surprise Len refused to take any form of payment – it was only after the event that he realised we were involved in community work and as the carnival had been our way of raising awareness he wanted to offer his services for free – the gesture of a real gent.

Not only that, but he said that if we ever wanted to borrow another model then all we had to do was ask. He also offered to put on a radio control helicopter flying display for free to our group – and so started a long friendly relationship with one of my hero's.

Soon after the carnival, Len invited me round to see where he built the models. This was a great opportunity to see how the great man planned and built his amazing machines. Len doesn't use kits – every component making up his helicopters is designed and built from scratch with the exception of engine and electronics.

In my mind I could see a large, modern, well laid out workshop with areas for design, fabrication and of course a large test area. Once again my perception could not have been more wrong. For those that have never visited Len and Olive you may be surprised to learn that they do not live in a mansion but in a small, semi-detached house on an estate built just after the 2nd world war. He and Olive have lived there most of their married lives and it is where they raised their family.

As you enter the tiny entrance hall, you notice a long glass-fronted wall cabinet stuffed full of trophies that Len has won over the years. As you head up the stairs towards the modelling room (a small 3m x 3m bedroom) there are various bits of helicopter hanging from the ceiling as there is no where else to put them.

The room is tiny with hundreds of small boxes that hold various bits and pieces, most of which have been collected over his many years of building world-class models. Of course this isn't the only place where Len does his modelling. The other place is a shed in the back garden which again is small and measures 4 metres x 2.5 metres. And that's about it. Out of these two places come some of the most exquisite accurate scale models that are often larger when assembled than the rooms he builds them in. Models that are among the best in the world.

But it isn't just the models that are inspirational. Len has a wealth of experience that he's able to pass on to those who want to listen. And then there are the stories – many of which are included in this book. A book that will amaze you and make you feel that anything is possible.

Michael Coveney, March 2011

1: Starting Out

I've always liked a challenge. Life can be very boring if everything you do is straightforward. The knowledge that something is either difficult or even impossible has always caused something deep within me to rise up and show that it can be done. It doesn't matter if the subject is outside of my experience, skill level or knowledge; being told that 'you won't be able to' is like waving a red flag at a bull. The more difficult the task, the more I want to take it on. It's this mindset and determination to meet every challenge that has brought me through my life and helped me achieve much of the success I have enjoyed in the hobby of radio controlled helicopters.

You may be one of those people who think they could never build a scale model, let alone build one to a high enough standard to win a competition. That's what I used to think but by breaking down what you are trying to accomplish into simple, smaller tasks, it's surprising what you can achieve. As I look back over my modelling career that started in 1968, I still find it hard to take in the amount of success I've had. I've won 21 national titles and over 500 individual competitions which, given my background and limited financial resources, should never have happened. But it is the challenge that spurs me on and helps me to overcome obstacles that at times seem insurmountable.

The early years

I was born on 28th May 1942 in Herne Bay, Kent – a quiet seaside resort on the South Coast of England that was popular through the 1950's and 60's but although this may sound idyllic, I didn't get to enjoy its many coastal pleasures. The reason was that my father who served in the Royal Artillery – eventually becoming a Sergeant Major – was continually being posted to different locations, which meant that our family were always on the move. As well as my father, my family consisted of my mother, two brothers and one sister. We were a fairly close family but it's sad that we were to drift apart as we grew older.

I must hold the record for the number of schools attended – 32 in all of which I was expelled from two of them, but more of that later. Some of the postings were abroad. I can remember at the age of eight being in Egypt where it was so hot that I spent most of my time in shorts and t-shirt. It was also around this time that I first became interested in the hobby of model flying that was to become the major part of my life.

It started with building balsa wood gliders, although I didn't have access to a model shop or even suitable model kits. There was something about flight I found fascinating, so I decided to design and build my own which provided many hours of pleasure to someone who spent most of his time alone. This was the 1950's when world events following the war were still unsettled. And as it turned out, Egypt was one of the more volatile areas of the world at that time. When the Suez crisis arose we had to be evacuated along with other military families back to the UK. I can still remember vividly seeing a dead body on the side of the road as we were being driven back to Cairo on our way 'home'.

Back in England I went through a succession of schools but my interests were never that well appreciated by my teachers. On one occasion while at boarding school, I had gotten into control-line model flying. This was before radio control and the only way of keeping some form of control over a model was to have it attached by wires to the wings. The weather wasn't good outside so I thought it would be good to fly it in the dormitory. Unfortunately the teachers didn't agree and I was expelled which suited me as I hadn't liked being there.

My second expulsion came when I was in a school in Larkhill, Wiltshire. I was 14 and had done something wrong, although I can't remember what it was. I was canned for my misdeed but when my brother found out he went to the teacher and hit him for which he was expelled. This made me mad and even more rebellious. Not long after I found some live .22 bullets on a firing range and took them into school. As you would expect of someone my age, I wanted to see if I could 'set them off', so I dropped bricks onto them and to my surprise one went off and shot a hole through a window. I joined my brother.

My older brother was a big influence on my early life. Soon after his expulsion he joined the Royal Artillery like our father, and signed up as a junior leader in Nuneaton. After a year he was posted to Germany. In 1958 I signed up with the same regiment, mainly because I had nothing else to do, and joined him after lying about my age (15 and a half as opposed to 16).

I was in the army for eight years and would have stayed longer but my time was cut short following a run-in with the commanding officer. I was a lance corporal and had gone on leave with one of my men. On the way back to the barracks the rear wheel bearing on my car broke up. This caused the brake pads to overheat which in turn boiled away the brake fluid jamming the brakes on. It took us some time to fix with the result that we were one hour late back at camp.

My brother was in command of the guardhouse who, on our return, put me on a charge. Because I was also responsible for making one of my men late, the charge was serious and I was offered the option of a court martial or to be punished by my Commanding Officer. I knew it wasn't my fault so I opted for the court martial. However the investigating officer claimed the car was fine and I was found guilty, stripped of my rank and sentenced to 10 days in jail. I felt I had been stitched up and as it coincided with an option to renew my stay in the army I thought 'why bother?'. I now regret leaving when I did, as if I had stayed on, I would have qualified for a good pension.

Married life

After leaving the army in 1966 I went to live with my father in Maidstone Kent. He was a chauffeur for the construction company McAlpine. I had a job at Rochester open-air swimming pool as superintendent, which was a great cushy job – all I had to do was to make sure there was no one at the bottom of the pool. Little did I know that the person I was to marry often sat on the hill overlooking the pool to have lunch.

I first met Olive on a blind date. At that time I had a Ford Zephyr Zodiac convertible – a real women puller. However, I wasn't looking for a long-term relationship, as all I wanted to do was to have a good time. On my youngest brother's 21st birthday, after much persistence from my parents, I arranged to take him out. To make it more palatable to me, my brother fixed me up with a blind date with someone who worked with him. It turned out to be Olive.

To begin with she didn't have that much of an impact on me, after all I was only interested in having fun and I had been road-ganged into having the date. We had a good evening and I dropped Olive off at her home and as far as I was concerned that was it. But three weeks later I just turned up at her house and asked her to go the pictures with me. And so it carried on.

Five months later I was watching television at her parents house when I said 'Let's go and see the vicar'. We had not discussed getting married and I had not proposed to her, but nothing seemed more natural. The next day we saw the vicar and six months after that we were married. People often think that whirlwind romances don't last, but Olive and I are testament to the contrary.

In those days not many people could afford a house, and the waiting list for council houses was very long. Olive's father was a builder and knew of houses owned by the council that were derelict. He managed to persuade them to let us have one for the princely sum of £1 and 4 old pence a week rent. The place was in such a mess that the council let us have it rent-free for 20 weeks. But after this time they decided to pull the house down and so had to re-house us, which meant we jumped right to the top of the council's house waiting list.

Ships in bottles

Both Olive and I didn't (and still don't) go out and socialise that much, so soon after getting married we wanted a hobby that we could do together that would also help with the housekeeping. We decided on putting ships into bottles. I've no idea why we did this, as we didn't know anyone who was into modelling be it planes, boats or anything else. The only thing that I can remember which spurred us on was that it was 'a bit of a challenge'.

As most people know, the ships are assembled outside of the bottle but with the masts collapsed so that they fit through the neck of the bottle. Once it's inside, strings attached to the mast are pulled to make the mast stand up to confound people on how it was done. I still have the first one I made.

To make things interesting we started making them to fit inside light bulbs and then car stoplight bulbs. The smallest one we ever made was in a 'grain of wheat' bulb – for those who've never seen one they measure 3mm x 1.5mm!

But after a while the challenge wasn't so great, so we decided to change from assembling them outside the bottle, to assembling them inside the bottle. This meant we had to paint every item outside of the bottle and then assembled them with special tweezers and glue sticks that we had adapted, inside the bottle. And it wasn't just the ship that had to be built. Each bottle had a 3-D backdrop such as a harbour scene, that showed off the boat.

Olive's role was in making the houses, the shore lines and the trees, while I concentrated on the ship itself. We would use any size bottle so each had to be made to fit – a skill I would come to use time and again in my future modelling life. This soon became a production line and we ended up with so many boats that we decided we might as well make this pay for itself. So I went to the off-license where we were getting our bottles from and offered them the finished models to sell to their customers.

Over a period of two years we must have sold over 30 ships, but towards the end it wasn't so much of a challenge, so we looked out for something else to do.

Radio control aeroplanes

Around this time (early 1970) I found a model shop about a quarter of mile away from the house called Sun Lane Engineering owned and run by modeller John Roper. This would eventually become the base for SLEC – a well known company of that time that made all kinds of plastic bits – control horns, clevises, hinges, etc - for the fast-growing hobby of radio control aircraft.

I went into the shop and told them that I wanted to get into radio control aeroplanes and asked them what they could do for me. I was sold a basic model kit with an on/off escapement driven by a rubber band. Basically the transmitter consisted of a single button which when pressed allowed a lever within the model to move to one side. In my model this would move the rudder to the left. When pressed twice the escapement would move the lever and hence the rudder to the right. A single press after either of the above would return the back to its originally position which theoretically would make the model fly straight. But the theory was very different from reality and I became very frustrated as I couldn't work out why I kept on crashing.

After a couple of months I went back to the model shop to buy another model as I was determined to fly. John in his wisdom sold me the favourite model of that year – a Keil Kraft Super 60. Most of the older modellers reading this book will remember this famous model that was loosely based on a high-wing aircraft and powered by a 35 size glo engine.

Proportional radio control had just come out which provided much more control over the more common 'on/off' escapement that was available, so I put this into the model – they were interesting years. Within a month I had the model built and, following the instructions supplied, balanced the wings.

I had never read any of the hobby magazines on the subject as it never interested me, so I joined the local model flying club in Gravesend and looked for someone to teach me to fly.

I arrived at the field, armed with my brand new (and expensive) Super 60. It wasn't too long before someone approached me who said they would teach me to fly. Even in those days I had a bit of a wise head so I thought that before letting him fly my model I would wait to see how he flew other peoples. I didn't have to wait long as he was soon at the controls of another person's model, which he crashed. And then he crashed another model, which made me very nervous.

I had spent a fortune on my model and I wasn't about to let anyone else apart from me destroy it. It seemed to me that this person was teaching himself to fly at the expense of other people – after all these were early days in proportional radio control systems. I decided not to let him or anyone else fly my model but instead to come back another day when no one else was there and do it all by myself.

While at the field I had been watching other people flying and taking note of what they were doing. It seemed quite obvious – left was left, up was up, and that sort of thing – surely it couldn't be that hard. So I went home and planned to go back another day when hopefully no one would be there.

The day soon came and when I arrived at the flying field it was perfect – a slight wind and best of all, no one was there. I thought – great – let's go for it. I nervously assembled the Super 60, which meant attaching the main wings via rubber bands and making sure all the control surfaces were connected. I filled up the tank with fresh fuel and connected the glo-plug to the 1.5 volt battery. With a few flicks of the finger the engine spluttered into life.

Without any delay the model trundled down the airstrip getting faster and faster and finally leaping into the air. It just seemed to float, wings level, a steady climb out and looking absolutely superb. Everyone had told me that I shouldn't do this on my own – but I couldn't understand what all the fuss was about. They told me it would crash – but this model just took off and flew so perfectly level I couldn't understand why everyone was so jittery.

It got to about 30 feet and the engine started to cough. I thought – ok don't panic, just leave it there – but it carried on coughing and then the engine shut down. The model gradually sank to the ground and to my surprise landed smoothly. I walked over to the model and picked it up. On inspecting the engine and airframe closely I couldn't find anything wrong with it so I thought I'd go back and do it again.

It was at this point I noticed that although I had switched the transmitter on, I had completely forgotten about turning on the receiver. My first flight hadn't been under my control after all – it had been flying all by itself. I decided at that point to go home, feeling totally drained but also very fortunate that I still had the model. I had been really lucky – if it hadn't been for the engine failing it would have probably flown away over the River Thames to Tilbury. Given the amount of money it had cost me, I would not have replaced it. And who knows, I may never have ended up moving onto model helicopters.

For my second flight I had someone stand beside me to make sure I did everything right.

2: Radio Control Helicopters

With the right guidance it didn't take me long to master radio-control flight of model airplanes. There's something exciting about seeing a model that you have personally built – even though it may be from a commercial kit – take to the air and fly under your control. In some ways the model becomes your way of being free from the laws of gravity and to move unfettered through the air like a bird.

The Super 60 was joined by an Astro Hog which had a low wing and gave me experience of using ailerons.   I also started experimenting in changing the models from standard. I converted the Super 60 to aileron control and put a 61 engine in it. That really made it fly!

But as with model ships, the challenge of radio-control flight was beginning to wane when a friend of mine said "Why don't we build a radio-controlled helicopter?" My initial reaction was "don't be stupid". This was still in the early 1970s when helicopter kits hadn't been thought of and only one or two people had even attempted such a complex feat of engineering. I told my friend that no one else had managed to build one so what makes him think we could, and if we did, where would we start? "Well", he said in his naïve manner, "It's very straightforward – we just copy a full size one."

Basically neither of us had a clue – and not only that, we hadn't even got basic machine tools such as a lathe or the experience of using one. Another major obstacle was the connection to a servo - you couldn't buy 'ball-links', which today are essential to controlling the moving parts on a helicopter. But it didn't stop us – after all it was 'a challenge'. And given the complexity involved, it is perhaps the greatest challenge for any model maker to build one from scratch!

We decided on building a Hughes 300, which seemed pretty straightforward as it didn't have much of a fuselage. What it did have we made from fibreglass. To power the rotor blades we used a Merco 61 engine with two glo-plugs but as this was designed for use at the front of an airplane where there is plenty of air passing over the cylinder to keep it cool, we had to incorporate a fan in the design of the mechanics.

With a helicopter there has to be some sort of clutch as the rotor blades should be stationary at engine tick-over but as the revs rise then the blades need to start turning. We solved this problem by using a clutch from a lawnmower driven by a chain from the engine. The blades however go at a much slower speed than the engine so we had to make a gearbox. This was done by bolting together two slabs of metal which enclosed the gears. The gears themselves came from various scrap metal yards and from the parts supplier Moffats. At that time we didn't have any moulding capabilities so the gears where meshed together by carefully filing the sides of the gearbox as well as the gears themselves until they fitted.

The tail drive was ordinary piano wire which given its shape (oval and not round) caused all sorts of vibration problems. The main rotor blades were made from hardwood leading edge and a balsa trailing edge. This was sand-sealed and covered in Fablon – a popular self-adhesive covering for use on kitchen work surfaces.

While we were doing this we had heard that Kavan, Graupner and Schluter in Europe, Jim Morley in the UK and Ernie Huber in the US, were also trying to build helicopters. Schluter eventually became the first to successfully hover a model helicopter and the news spread like wild fire around the modelling world.

After six months our model was ready to test fly. It was 80cm wide, 180cm long and 80cm high. It wasn't exactly a scale model but the dimensions were in proportion to the full size model. It even had a fully collective pitch (something that very few others were trying) – purely because the full size we copied had that. But despite all of this, the damn thing wouldn't get off the ground.

We initially thought that it was too heavy so we drilled the tail boom until it resembled a Gatling gun –there were so many holes it was untrue. We then played around with different rotor and tail blades – it was a question of 'suck it and see' as we had no idea of what they should be like. We knew we needed lift so we produced blades with an under-camber along the wing just like a glider. They were made of obichee wood on the leading edge with balsa on the trailing edge and just painted with no reinforcing or anything. We got a piece of wood, shaped it to the camber we wanted, glued sandpaper to it and just rubbed it down and down. We did the same with the tail blades.

For paddles we used 5cm diameter tin cans – they looked stupid but they turned out to be highly effective. I attempted to read up on the theory of helicopters but it didn't make much sense - in fact it still doesn't make much sense to me even today. We took the front off the model so it looked just like a shoe box – it certainly didn't resemble any full size helicopter but still it wouldn't fly.

We tried for over a year to get this thing to hover and then one day it just jumped into the air – it was just about controllable but it leaned to one side. When we pushed in forward we had the swash-plate configured to go forward and to the right – hence it veered off and we couldn't steer it . It turned out that we had the theory all wrong. It wasn't the helicopter at fault for not flying – it was me the pilot who didn't know how to fly.

I'm often asked if we crashed a lot during this time as most of the test flights were in a small back garden that measured 5 metre x 8 metre long. To be honest I can't remember ever crashing although we hit the clothesline pole a few times. After a while we transferred the test flights to my mates house where we hit their clothesline pole as well.

Above: Len's flying lawnmower!

Below: Len's very first helicopter built from scratch - long before kits were available

Above: Len's very first kit was a Schluter Cobra - this one belongs to a friend Barry Baker

Below: A Schluter Helibaby

First kit helicopter kit

It was very exciting to finally get our model into the air but by this time Schluter was marketing a kit – a Cobra – so I thought we might as well give up on ours and go and buy one.

I went to the UK importer who told me that he wouldn't have them for at least another six months – but I knew they were available from other sources. So I got in contact with a model shop in Southern Ireland to buy one. The shop owner said that it would be no problem to get hold of the kit but that I would be charged a lot of import duty to get it into the UK.

I thought about it and asked him if he could break the machine down into pieces. The fuselage was over 2 metres long, so I asked him to put masking tape around the fuselage in four or five sections and then cut along those sections and send me the kit in pieces. I reassured him that I had the capability of fibre glassing it all back together again when I received it. The idea was that parcels from outside the UK under a certain weight and size, were not looked at by Customs and hence I wouldn't incur import duty.

Soon after placing the order, the postman knocked on my door saying he had a parcel for me and would I mind signing for it – there was nothing to pay which was great. In the box was a rotor head. The following day the postman knocked again with two more parcels – I signed for them and found the gearbox and under carriage.

The middle part of the fuselage turned up the following day along with the tail rotor. For the next week or so I had regular visits from the postman who would often say "Here's another birthday present". I finally got all the bits and pieces of the kit without paying a penny in import duty. Of course I had to pay postage but that was much cheaper than paying the duty.

Once I had received everything, I put the fuselage together by fibre glassing the join on the inside. It turned out to be as good as new, except a little heavier. I then fitted the mechanics and the undercarriage. The end result looked and was known as 'a praying mantis'. It was 2 metres wide by 2 metres long with a rotor diameter of 2 metres. It stood 1 metre high off the ground and had a three pointed training under carriage, which was wise as it prevented the tail rotor from hitting the ground and gave it a wide stable platform.

First flight

I took the completed model to the sports field in Gravesend, where my friends and I flew. I fuelled up the gleaming Cobra and set it down with some trepidation – it had cost a lot of money, which to me represented five months worth wages. I had about five years experience in flying aircraft and thought that a helicopter shouldn't be too difficult to fly. The Cobra was a fixed pitch machine, which meant that as the throttle was opened up then the machine would rise due to the lift generated by the rotor. Likewise, if the throttle was closed then the machine would descend as the rotor 'slowed' down. This was quite daunting as I had been used to a fully collective pitch on my own design where these two controls – throttle and up/down control - were separated.

With my heart in my mouth I fired up the engine in the model and placed it on the flight line. I took several steps back and opened up the throttle. The pitch of the engine rose rapidly as did the speed of the rotor head where the blades whipped round like a demented circular saw. As I stood there transfixed on the model it took off … l/2 metre in the air, then 1 metre, then 2 metres, then 6 metres and didn't stop there. It kept going up because I had forgotten to cut back on the throttle. For those of you that have flown helicopters you'll know that you need a lot of power to get into the air but once it's off the ground you need to reduce the power so that it hovers or it will just keep climbing.

But I could not shut the throttle – something inside me kept telling me that if I cut the throttle it would fall out of the sky and hit the ground – hard. But as I sweated and concentrated on the model, I noticed it was now travelling forward just like an aeroplane. So I decided to control it like an aeroplane and fly a circuit - after all I could fly circuits with an aeroplane and I didn't think there would be too much difference with the helicopter. To my surprise and great relief round it went – just like my aeroplanes. It just seemed natural and given the size of the model I didn't have any problem with orientation.

After completing a couple of circuits the next problem loomed large in my mind – how on earth was I going to get this thing down! I just kept repeating and repeating it – how on earth am I going to get it down – but unbeknown to me I was talking out loud. My mate who was standing next to me heard me and said, "You know how to land aeroplanes – land it like an aeroplane". Not a bad idea I thought, so as I was flying the circuits I gradually started to shut down the throttle. It was getting lower and lower and I thought if I don't get it down soon we're going to run out of fuel. My eyes became a one-armed bandit – I could see pounds shillings and pence rolling around in my head – and quite a few hard words from the missus if I went home with the helicopter in a bag of bits.

So I got it fairly low and thought why don't I just glide it in like an aeroplane. So that's what I did. I reduced the throttle, just as you would with an aeroplane, keeping the wings, or in my case the rotor blades, level. And it worked. The model flared out just above the landing strip - the front leg of the training undercarriage was up in the air just higher than the rear legs which were about 1 metre off the ground. The two rear wheels then touched down and the whole model just sank down to the ground.

The people around me were up in the air over what I had just achieved but I was absolutely drained. However I went home very happy. It was an experience that nobody could ever forget.

First helicopter sales

Around this time I became involved in helping out at the Kent School of Model Flying. The school was a response to the demand of people coming to our club who wanted to learn to fly model aircraft. It was started by two friends of mine – John Salt and Alan Withy.

The way it would work is that the school owned a number of models. These were made of foam and had thin obechee veneer on the underbelly instead of an undercarriage. They would be hand launched and landed on grass. In order to make the flying sessions continuous, we had two trestle tables with three aeroplanes, two pilots and one helper.

On one table there would be a plane in a jig with its engine already running. A customer would come in, pay his fee (£1 per 10 minute flight), and take hold of the transmitter buddy box. An instructor would take the plane and throw it into the air to start the session.

While that one was flying, the helper would start up a second plane so that it was ready to go. At the end of a flying session, the helper would take the model just flown, clean it up and refuel it so it was ready to be started for its next flight. It was just like a conveyor belt.

A crucial part of making this a success was the way in which the instructor and pupil's transmitters were connected together, now known as a 'buddy box' system. This enabled the instructor to take over full control of the model from the pupil when necessary, for example when taking off and landing, or when the pupil had gotten themselves into trouble. Up until this time there were no such systems available, and I believe it was Alan Withey in conjunction with Skyleader radio who came up with the solution. By pressing a button on the instructors transmitter, control would be passed to the pupil, until it was released when control then passed back to the instructor. It worked very, very well and meant the pupils didn't crash, so it saved them a lot of money as well as giving them more flying time.

The reason why I became involved was that John wasn't around that much due to his work commitments as a full-size pilot, and I was asked if I could help out. As a result I spent most of my weekends for the next two years, with Alan teaching people to fly.

We were very busy and would be teaching all day. We had people from all walks of life come to the flying field. Some would walk in, others would get a bus, some would come on a bike, while others came by car. We even had people who came by Rolls Royce.

When there was a lull in the flying I used to fly my helicopters. One day while flying my Kavan Jet Ranger, a gentleman come up to me and say "How much do you want for that". I told him that it was not for sale to which he replied "Everything is for sale if the price is right". That taught me a lesson that I was not to forget. So I quoted him a price. A few moments later while still flying he put a cheque into my back pocket.

I said "The price doesn't include the radio". "How much do you want for that", he replied. At the end of the day I went home with two cheques and no helicopter or radio.

When I got home I started to wonder what I would fly the following weekend. So with the money I was given for the model, I went and purchased another helicopter kit and built that within two weeks. Soon after, someone else bought that and so I had to get another kit – and so it went on.

Kit building

Over the next few months I bought a range of models as I wanted to get as much experience in trying out different helicopters as I possibly could, but without dipping into the housekeeping money. Fortunately, the money I received in selling my models was sufficient to pay for all my expenses.

This experience helped me in a couple of ways. First it helped immensely with the speed at which I could build models, something that was to benefit me throughout my whole model life. Second, I learned to distinguish between good and bad helicopter designs, again something that was to help me in building my own models.

I must have tried all the major model manufacturers, but my favourite – the one I always came back to and in my opinion the best – was Schluter.

Unlike some manufacturers, the kits came with parts that didn't need much finishing. For example, with Morley helicopters you had to make the clutch, drill the holes and make assemblies from many different parts. They were known as the 'birds nest kit' because they were so full of bits and pieces – you often had five bits to do the same job that other companies would do in two. On the positive side though, Morley did have a good range that sold well as they were much cheaper than anyone else.

Other manufacturers like Kavan, would continually send you updates to their helicopter. During one period I remember getting a new gearbox output shaft every fortnight, I must have received about 15 shafts in all. Many would think this was good customer service but I couldn't help thinking why they couldn't get it right in the first place.

To me, reliability and the availability of spares are the most important thing because if you crash today, you want to be in the air tomorrow. If the kit importer says they don't have any main shafts, then you're not in the air until they have. Of course that doesn't usually happen nowadays as there are so many shops selling helicopters, but in those days you were lucky to find four shops selling them.

With Schluter, I found a manufacturer that had good kits, great design – they had oil filled gear boxes as standard, and spare parts that were easily available. This became even more important due to the number of kits I was getting through.

I could guarantee to sell at least one, ready-made helicopter a month. They were all fitted out and came with a nice paint job. All the customer had to do was supply the transmitter. I didn't skimp on the price but I didn't overcharge. I made enough on each sale to buy everything new again. I bought kits from model shops, sometimes through importers while at other times it was directly from the manufacturer. I was fortunate in that I was in the hobby from the beginning and was well known to many of the manufacturers. This helped me to get things a little cheaper than the average modeller could get.

After a while, many of my customers were people I didn't know. My fame had spread through the word of satisfied customers and so I would often get phone calls from strangers. Some of my customers would come back to me for more advanced models as their flying progressed.

One particular model, a Schluter Estrom, I actually bought back nine times. I loved that model – it was on floats when I first sold it. The person who bought it came back to me a year later saying he couldn't afford to fly it anymore, as children had come along. He asked me if I would buy it back – so I did and soon found another customer for the model. That buyer then came back a little later – and so it went on. With this model it happened nine times and every time I bought it back, it would be rubbed down, repainted and usually improved in some way. I don't know where it is now but I'm sure it's still out there, somewhere.

At this time, Olive wasn't that involved in building the models. We had young children and so most of her time was spent in looking after them.

3: Going It Alone

In the army, I was always being told what to do and where to go - I didn't have a choice. So, when I left I felt like rebelling against any form of control over my life. This didn't help me in the jobs that followed as they took me back to my army days in that I was again being told what to do. I came to the inevitable conclusion that I had to work for myself, much against the wishes of my father-in-law.

His view was that in working for someone else you could go home at 5pm and not worry about work until the following day, but to me it felt like a prison where I had lost my freedom. I figured that the best thing about working for yourself was that you didn't have to do anything anyone asked you. Of course you had to earn money but at least you had the choice of when and where you worked, and to me that was extremely important.

But how do you make enough money out of a hobby to live, let alone to have a comfortable life? This was another challenge and one that would take several years and many hard lessons to overcome.

First sponsor

During the 1970's I worked as a motor mechanic at a local Ford dealer – J Davy – in Gravesend. When I wasn't at work, I was building helicopters for other people but after a while a couple of things were troubling me. First I could see that different manufacturers had different strengths but no one had what I considered to be the ideal model. I was already known as 'Mr. Modifyer' as I was always modifying the kits to make them better and to match the way I liked to fly. What I wanted to do was take the best bits from each and make my own bits for those areas I thought no one did a good job. But this brought me to my second issue – I was only just covering my costs, I couldn't even afford basic machine tools like a lathe. I decided then and there that I had to get a sponsor as I needed to do this hobby better than I was currently doing it, but for which I couldn't afford.

I became quite an expert in performing aerobatics - loops and rolls – which led me to winning more and more competitions, first local events and then national events. During the late 1970's I dominated the British Nationals in F3C for radio control helicopter aerobatics. This was to get me noticed by Max Coote of Ripmax who wanted to sponsor me. In our hobby at that time, sponsorship didn't usually involve money but you would get parts and kits as well as free travel to different places to show off your skills as well as the sponsor's products. I was given a Ripmax radio, and although it wasn't that much, at least it was one expense I didn't have to worry about.

Going inverted

Then Schluter launched a model that was to change my life and open up the way for me to make a full-time living from model helicopters. The Schluter Heliboys was advertised as being aerobatic – and it certainly was. The main reason for this was its 'pod and boom' design that made it light and mechanically simple. In fact this was one of the first ever pod and boom model as kits up to this point were based on full size helicopters with fuselages that covered the engine and mechanics. It was also easy to modify – with a few tweaks you could increase the throw on the paddles and rotor blades making it very manoeuvrable which suited my style of flying. Fortunately the rest of the mechanics could handle the stress that this placed on them.

One day a friend of mine said to me "Why don't you fly inverted?" This was the one manoeuvre that most people thought was impossible, due to the many technical challenges that are involved. For example, when upright the spinning rotor generates lift by ensuring the blades have a positive pitch. But to fly inverted, the direction of lift must be reversed or the helicopter will 'suck' itself into the ground. This means changing the pitch of the blades to be negative. However, engine speed is typically connected to the pitch of the blades. The more positive the pitch the higher the engine speed, which is fine for flying normally. But when, and only when, flying inverted we need to maintain engine speed while decreasing pitch. With today's computer controlled transmitters this isn't a problem, but at that time transmitters were very basic and there was no simple way to make this happen.

Another problem is to do with the flow of fuel to the engine. In those days, fuel was picked up from the bottom of the tank via a pipe that had a weighted end. Air vents were placed at the top of the tank to ensure a vacuum doesn't occur as the tank empties otherwise fuel would stop flowing to the engine. The only trouble is that when inverted, fuel would block the air vents causing the fuel supply to the engine to be disrupted. The last thing you need when inverted is for the engine to splutter or stop!

As well as the technical challenges, there are challenges facing the pilot in how he sees and reacts to the attitude of the model. As already mentioned, transmitters were simple affairs and they didn't have reversing switches. This meant that if you did get the model inverted, then for control purposes you had to reverse your brain for some of the functions. For example, to ascend normally means that the pitch stick has to move up, but when inverted, to go 'up' involves moving the Pitch stick 'down'. This of course assumes that engine speed is being controlled independent of pitch position.

To add to the confusion, when inverted, turns to the left via the tail rotor now go to the right while forward and back cyclic direction is also reversed. But bizarrely, left and right cyclic direction stay the same. Many would-be helicopter pilots struggle to 'reverse' controls when the helicopter turns in front of them when flying the right way up, flying inverted greatly increases complexity. But these were challenges to relish and so I came home and thought about what I had to do.

As mentioned above, most helicopter setups have the engine speed on the same control as the rotor blade pitch. The control is usually arranged so that at low engine speed there would be negative pitch on the blades that would gradually increase to positive pitch at full engine speed. (It's actually not quite that simple as the engine speed is not directly proportional to pitch but we can ignore this for our purposes). To achieve both normal and inverted flight, I knew that I had to have full throttle at both the low and full pitch positions, and at the mid throttle point I needed zero pitch. As far as pitch was concerned, I knew I needed to have +8 degrees to fly normally and -8 degrees to fly inverted.

After puzzling over how I could do this, I put the throttle onto a switch so that it was either 'full on' or 'tick-over', leaving the 'throttle' stick on the transmitter to operate just the pitch of the blades. This made the model quite hairy to fly, so you had to know where the zero degree pitch was.

I solved this by placing a groove on the transmitter 'throttle stick' ratchet so that as the stick moved to zero degrees there was a 'click' that could be felt through the stick. This meant I could now invert the model and use the remaining 'throttle stick' to put in negative pitch. This worked quite well. Of course while inverted I had to 'remember' to reverse the other controls for left and right manually. This was fairly easy to do provided you concentrated and no one spoke to you.

The first time I went inverted, the model did a couple of pirouettes and a lot of backward flying. This was because I had forgotten to reverse the cyclic control to make it go forward, but I didn't crash. In fact I can't ever remember crashing through pilot error but the engine spluttered a few times due to fuel starvation

To fix the engine problem I first of all put in top and bottom vents to the tank and fitted them with one way valves to stop the fuel leaking out. It didn't work. What I needed was a constant fuel supply so I decided to pressurise the tank – something that wasn't done in those days. I didn't know how to do this but after experimenting with connections to the manifold and exhaust pipe, I finally got there.

I soon perfected inverted flight. I wasn't aware of anyone else who had done this although I learned later that Mike Mass and Ernie Huber in the US had also managed to achieve inverted flight. I'm not sure which of us was 'first', but I was certainly the first in Europe.

My sponsor, Max Coote, was keen to show off my talents and so it was arranged that I would fly inverted for the first time in public at the Sandown Park Symposium. I planned to show this off by flying in a mirror formation i.e. one helicopter above another, with the one on top inverted. A dear friend of mine, Terry Hobday, was to fly the 'normal' way up but because of the very real likely-hood that a crash would destroy both models, I was to supply both machines. This provided ample incentive to get it right.

Above: Trimming a machine one handed - don't try this at home!

Below: Going inverted.

Above: Olive gets to grip with one of Len's airplanes - it's large scale of course

Below: Olive and daughter Tina at a trade show. Len's F3C model 'Swift' is on display

Helicopter blades

During this time I started to make my own tail and rotor blades as I felt the commercial ones just weren't good enough for my style of flying. Model kits came with wooden blades but if they were not sealed properly they could get damp and swell up. This meant that when they got dirty from the oil residue from the engine, they couldn't be soaked to clean them up. They were also time-consuming to make as they would have to be made up with reinforcing strips, covered and painted, which was a lot of work. Another problem was they were not that strong along the length so in aerobatic manoeuvres they could twist which then affected pitch and ruined the flight. However, blades made out of fibreglass could overcome all of these problems, so I decided to make my own.

As with most things in life, this turned out to be more difficult than I'd expected. I had already made and repaired a few fuselages, so I knew how to fibreglass but this was only in polyester as I didn't know about epoxy resin. The rotor blades I was using were made of wood and flexed a lot, so to stiffen them up I coated them with a polyester resin and fine cloth which was then sanded down. These were much better but the C of G was now in the wrong place, which led to instability. To cure this I decided to make them completely out of fibre glass. I had no experience of doing this but the most logical way to me was to make them in two halves - top and bottom – and join them.

I made the plugs by sanding a wooden blade to the final shape I wanted and covered it with polyester resin reinforced fibreglass to make two moulds - a top and a bottom. These moulds were then polished to help with the release process and a gel coat put in place that would become the surface of the new blade. Cloth and polyester resin were then laid onto the gel coat. For the leading edge I had a friend with a spindle moulding machine make some up out of obeche veneer. These were quite heavy so I decided not to put anything into the trailing edge. While the cloth layers were still wet , the top and bottom half's were clamped together and left to cure overnight. I was pleasantly surprised when the first blades came out as they looked quite good.

Unfortunately as the blades spun up I could see them start to ripple which I concluded was due to nothing being in the trailing end. I thought about putting in wing ribs like those in an aeroplane but rejected this as it would be a very long process. I then tried injecting two-part foam into the hollow blade but as well as filling the cavity it also caused the blade to bulge destroying the profile I wanted to achieve. In the end I managed to solve this problem by shaping a piece of foam and placing it in the mould as the skins were being created.

I now had to find a way of weighting the front of the blades in order to get the C of G in the right place. Initially I made a groove in the leading edge and filled it up with lead. This seemed to work as on the next test flight the blades tracked true with no vibrations. But as I went to fly a circuit the blades disintegrated in mid-air causing the helicopter to blow up. The hole

I had drilled for attaching the blades to the blade grip had split causing the blade to fail, so I knew it had to be reinforced.

Despite all these setbacks, they were a blessing in disguise in that they taught me how to build a rotor blade that was not only efficient but was also strong. The revised design included a leading edge spar made out of fibreglass that encapsulated a lead weight and a reinforced root. These were a complete success and I started to win more and more competitions. As well as making the machine more stable, my own design blades made auto-rotations a dream. I won these competitions easily as I could really load up the blades to create so much inertia that you could hover the helicopter just above the ground with no engine and have a cup of tea!

This success generated many enquiries for the blades. First my mates asked me for a set, so I started making and selling them at my local club field. This then extended into model shows and I started to think that this could be the way to finally make a living out of the hobby.

The decision was soon made for me as I became redundant from my 'day job' and I went on the dole. I didn't like the idea of not working so I thought why don't I make rotor blades and see how it goes. I had a good family behind me and I knew that if I got into trouble, I could always count on them. But I never did – I sold enough blades to keep us going. I was selling rotor blades for £25 a set for a 35 size helicopter – 15 years later they were still £25 – I never put our prices up.

I started selling 10 sets a month, then 20, then 40 a month. My best month was 50 sets. Most of our business came through word-of-mouth but after only a short time I was selling direct to customers as well as to retailers. And it just wasn't in the UK, the business extended to sales in the USA, Canada, New Zealand and Japan. I didn't employ anyone – it was just Olive and I making them. We would have up to 12 moulds for each blade design but as there were small marks in each mould we would make sure that we paired up blades from the same mould. We created our own production line. Olive would polish the moulds while I made the leading edge. Olive would cut the cloth to shape and we would both lay up a blade half each. These would then be joined and left to cure overnight.

Business was good. For example we would go along to the Sandown symposium with 300 pairs of blades and sell every one of them. We didn't make a fortune but it got us by for the next 20 years. Towards the end though, the market started to get competitive. When we started there were only three companies that made blades but now everyone seemed to be making them. Both the design and quality had improved to the extent that our 'home produce' seemed irrelevant. We also found it boring so we decided to finish the blade making business and look for something else to do. To bring matters to a head, one mad day in the late 1990s we picked up all the blade moulds and took them down the tip and got rid of them. There was no going back. I still make my own blades but not for anyone else.

Scale Fuselages

We still needed to generate an income so we looked around at what we could do next. At this time I was making my own scale competition fuselages but people would often ask me to make them one. It didn't take me long to realise that after making the mould, I could turn out a high quality fuselage in two days and sell it for £400. This was so much easier and faster to do that making the equivalent amount from a set of rotor blades. It was also a lot more fun, so from the end of 1998, LM Blades became Len Mount Scale Fuselages and Olive and I were back in business.

I've always had an interest in scale models. In the early days I made scale aeroplanes from the World War 1 and World War 2 era, plus a couple of civilian planes. Then when I started building helicopters I went straight to building scale machines. Not content to just have a scale body I would start putting in seats and instrument panels. But as I got more into F3C aerobatic competitions and the need to continually practice, I dropped scale model building.

Between 1977 and 1997 I won 15 national F3C aerobatic championships including the UK, Scottish, Irish and New Zealand. Competition at this level wasn't boring but it did get repetitious and it can easily take over your life. If you wanted to win you had to keep practicing and that meant being out in all weathers. But as I got older my reactions were getting slower so I had to practice even harder. Then one day I decided I had had enough and so I went back into scale modelling.

The contrast couldn't be more different. Whereas with aerobatics I would have to go out every day of the week to practice, with scale flying I could get by with just a weekly flight as the manoeuvres are relatively easy. Then there were the machines. With F3C I would need three machines in top condition, but with scale I just needed one. And finally there was the cost. With F3C I would get through five engines in a year at an equivalent cost of £1000, while I would use six gallons of fuel each week in practicing at a cost of over £4,000. F3C was a rich mans sport! However in scale, one engine would be sufficient and the fuel used would be no more than that used by a typical 'hobby' flier.

The only other major difference was in the building. With aerobatics you can 'buy' a model that is capable of winning, but in scale, winning requires something special that money can't buy. It requires an eye for detail, patience in making things in miniature, dedication and above all perseverance. Interestingly it needn't be expensive. All the scale detail on my models are made from scrap or everyday objects that cost pennies. But it is hard work and does take time.

My return to scale modelling was serious. I put in ash-trays complete with cigarette butts, seat belts that would 'click' shut and seats work along with working adjustable height mechanisms. My cockpits would have gauges that consist of miniature photographs of the real dial and even the flight joystick would move in conjunction with the rotor head. The rotor heads are exact duplicates of the original and so these are built from scratch along with the mechanics so I have enough room to add interior scale detail. Many of the scale details were things that no one would notice – hinges with micro screws, maps, cans of drink and the underwear for the pilot models. All were painstakingly researched and added to the model. The paint would be the exact paint used on the full-size aircraft, all markings on the aircraft would be present right down to any surface imperfections including any scratches.

In scale modelling there are two extremes. At the 'bottom end' there is 'stand off' scale where models are judged from a distance of 2 metres and so it's easy to get away with non-scale features or inaccuracies in the placement of hinges and body outline. At the top end – where I operate - the judges examine the model at close quarters and compare every part – both inside and outside – with photos taken of the original subject. This can take them up to 20 minutes and in most cases they can't find a single rivet or joint out of place. Not too many people model at this level, probably because of the time and dedication it requires. But for me, trying to achieve perfection is what drives me both in the building of the model and in the models flying characteristics. My models are built to fly – and I don't hold back when I fly them as many people who have seen me will testify. As result I am rarely beaten in scale competitions, which lead to enquiries about my supplying fuselages.

One of the first scale fuselages I built to market was the AH-1 Cobra, an attack helicopter manufactured by Bell. In looking at other helicopter kit manufacturers I noticed that there wasn't a large-scale model of the Cobra so I decided to build my own. I looked through some library books to find a suitable 3-view drawing, which I then scaled up on a photocopier to a size that would take a 23cc petrol engine. Fortunately around this time I had been invited to go to a show in Long Island, New York and while there I was invited to visit a military base that just happened to have a full size version. This enabled me to take a lot of close-up photos that helped to get the scale detail right. In all, the model including making the mould took around six months to build.

Over a period of eight years we produced nine different fuselages, all of which are still available today. Each kit would take around three to four months to develop. Some would be available as a straightforward fuselage while others would come with retracts and engine frames already installed ready to take the mechanics. Over the years I have built moulds for the N4 Dauphin, AS 355, BK117, Airwolf, Huey, Cobra, Rotorway, Kiowa, Scout, BO105, Hiller J10, Puma, Lynx, and a number of non-scale fuselages for my F3C models as well as various 'pod and boom' models.

By 2006 I had made just over 150 fuselages but as I was nearing retirement and with both my wife and myself falling ill, we decided to sell up. A close friend, Al Wert of Starwood Scale Models based in California, bought all the moulds and now operates this as part of his business. I still make one-off scale models either for my own pleasure or on a commission basis, but my days as a manufacturer are now well and truly over.

4: Trips and Tricks

I've always liked to travel – and I still do. There's something about packing a case and going to the airport – a sense of anticipation of what you're going to encounter in a 'foreign' world. Maybe it comes from my upbringing where we were always constantly moving home. By the time I was ten I had experiences of living abroad that must have been the envy of most people at that time. Flying inverted was the party trick that ensured my life in helicopters would also take me around the world.

My first trip abroad came courtesy of Ripmax – one of the largest importers of radio control equipment in the UK. At the time I was flying Schluter Heliboys that were imported by Ripmax. Max Coote – the owner of Ripmax - took me under his wing although he didn't sponsor me directly. He took me to various prestigious shows in the UK such as Woodvale. I wasn't paid, but I was given hotel rooms for myself and Olive, as well as petrol and living expenses. I could also get spares for my models so I guess you can say I was semi-sponsored.

As fame of my ability grew, so the offers to fly further away, grew. People wanted to see me fly inverted and it wasn't long before Max was taking me to fly in France, Belgium and Holland.

Delighting the French

One French trip that was particularly exciting for me, was when I responded to an invitation to fly at a club meeting in Nancy, France. Each year the club would award trophies in various categories such as the best beginner, the top club flyer and so on. They said that they would arrange accommodation for me but I didn't want to go alone so I asked the organisers that if I could take four friends with me, we would camp to save on expenses. They agreed and asked that we would all fly – me with my helicopter and my friends with their aeroplanes.

On arriving in Nancy, we were met by a reception committee that couldn't speak English. We couldn't speak French and so neither party could understand what the other were saying. However there seemed to be a common bond and unperturbed we went with them to the club flying field – and what a field it was. The flying field was well tended with safety fences to protect spectators. It had a clubhouse with restroom facilities, the like I had never seen in the UK at that time.

We were then invited into the club-house for something to eat – and what a feast that was. A five-course meal that would have put a lot of restaurants to shame. But still no one spoke a word of English. Then a good-looking school-teacher turned up who could speak English – she was to be our chaperone for the weekend. She told me that I was there to demonstrate inverted flying and that the club had opened up the event for free to the whole town.

On the Saturday I did a few flights and had a great time showing what the machine was capable of. That evening we had some fun with some foam gliders we had bought to which we attached torches so we could see where they were. Come the Sunday I was again asked to fly which I agreed to, but this time I didn't hold back. After flying around I went inverted and lowered the machine so that it was hovering, up side down, about 5cm off the ground. I then went down on one knee and took my hat off and waved to the crowd. They went wild.

Some people may think that this was being reckless – remember there were no computer radios in those days and most of the skill was in remembering to invert certain functions when flying upside down. But I had heavily modified the model so that it was far more stable than the kit it was built from.

On a second flight I got hold of some safety matches and wrapped the whole box onto a nail that was then stuck in the ground so that the match tips faced upwards. I then stuck some sandpaper to the blades of the helicopter. After taking off I went inverted and hovered lower and lower above the matches until the sandpaper struck the match tips. Poof – the matches ignited and the smoke from the ignition was blown out so all could see I had hit them. The reaction from the crowd was fantastic.

At the end of the day they came to award the prizes. I must admit I wasn't really listening as I couldn't understand French, when there was an unmistakable announcement that sounded like 'Mousier Mont'. Our chaperone told me I was wanted and took me up the steps onto the podium where I was awarded a trophy for the best demonstration flight of the weekend.

I was quite chuffed but as I turned around to walk away and the compare says "No,no. Come come" and hands me six bottles of wine. After receiving these I was walking down the podium steps when I hear "Mousier Mont, come come." This time it was for a prize based on feedback from the towns people of the best flight of the weekend. I got another trophy and another six bottles of wine.

I was on my way back down the steps when I hear "Mousier Mont …" And so it went on – towards the end I became quite emotional. I went up a total of six times that afternoon. The newspaper reporting on the event thought it was the best show they had ever been to, as did the mayor of the town. I had gained a total of six trophies and 36 bottles of wine.

I kept the best trophy for myself and I gave my companions a choice of what they wanted. We planned to share the wine. But on the way home Customs & Excise at Dover had other ideas. After declaring the trophies and the wine we were bringing back, we found we were two bottles over the limit. I told them that they could keep them but that wasn't allowed. Neither were we allowed to drink them there or pour them down a drain, so we had to pay import duty.

Still I had a whole case of wine. The only trouble was when I got home and took a sip, it was so vile that I couldn't stand it - it was just like vinegar. So I poured them all down the drain.

Rolling Around in Holland

On another occasion I was invited to go to a show organised by the model flying club Jupiter, based in Venlo, Holland. My models then were very aerobatic as I knew how to tune up all the linkages to get the control I wanted. This had to be done mechanically as there were no computer controlled transmitters in those days. The only gyros available were mechanical ones and I must admit I loved them. Although I didn't know too much on how they worked, I did know how to tweak them so that they were superior to anyone else's.

I was flying inverted when someone asked me how many rolls I could do. I said I had no idea. So I flew up and performed five consecutive rolls in a circuit in front of me. They then said 'Why don't you go for the Guinness book of records?" and I thought , OK.

I wasn't sure how many they wanted me to do so we agreed that I would do as many as I could on a full tank of fuel. All the committee members of the flying club were there, as well as the mayor and many other adjudicators. After doing 20 rolls the crowd were getting behind the attempt and started counting. I managed to do 80 consecutive rolls in 12 minutes – the only thing that stopped me was that I was knackered. The club wrote to the Guinness book of records asking them to accept the record but unfortunately they wouldn't as none of their representatives were present at the attempt. Despite the disappointment it was a lot of fun, however I would love to have gotten into the record books.

East European trip

Of course, it's not all fun as I found out in a trip to East Germany (as it was known in the 'cold-war' days). I had been in Germany competing in the Schluter Cup when a very scruffy looking guy came up and asked me if I would like to go to Budapest. "Where's that?", I asked. "It's in Hungary" he snapped back, as though everyone apart from me knew where it was. Despite the rebuff, I found the offer exciting as I had never been to Budapest, Hungary before – this would be another country on the notch of my belt.

"Sure", I said, "What would you like me to do?" "I want you to do some training for us", the man replied. "Ok – but it's up to the wife." So I went up to Olive and asked her if I could go to Budapest. The reason for asking is that I was doing so many trips away from home I thought it was unfair not to ask her. As always, Olive gave her blessing and so off I went to Budapest and did some training with three guys who wanted to learn to fly radio control helicopters. About a month later the person who invited me phoned me asked "I've got a secret project coming up for the military – I want a camera ship, can you make one for me?" "Oh that's no problem", I said, "but how are you going to pay for it." "We'll pay you when you get here", he replied. However that wasn't acceptable to me as I needed to make the model to hold the camera before going to Hungary. This was going to cost me, and as I didn't really know these people I wasn't prepared to risk my own money in case the whole thing fell threw. But the chap was determined to employ me so he made a special trip to Britain to give me some cash.

I only had two weeks to build the model, which wasn't long enough for me to design my own and so I went and bought a big 90 size Robbe helicopter that I adapted for the camera. Later on during the trip I found out that my contact wasn't happy with that as he wanted me to design something specific for the purpose. But you can't design a helicopter and then build the special parts required in just two weeks. My agreement with the people in Hungary was that I would build the model and fly it, while they would supply the camera. When the model was ready I phoned him and asked him what size camera he would be supplying. He gave me the measurements and I made a mock-up to make sure it would fit the model I had built.

So off I went to Budapest and into the hotel room that was booked by my contact. To my surprise he was already there. I asked him where the camera was to which he replied that it would be with us within a few minutes. Sure enough along came two guys with leather jackets and hefty boots with the camera. I thought the camera looked familiar and as it had bare wires instead of a connector, it dawned on me that this had just been taken off the wall outside the supermarket – it was the CCTV camera.

They wired it all up and transmitted the pictures to a TV set – but the picture was rotating and wouldn't stay still. On seeing this, one of the guys went out and half an hour later came back with another camera. That didn't work either. I thought to myself that this doesn't feel that comfortable and began to wish that I had never taken the trip on.

Another person came along holding a camera that was 8cm square by 5cm deep complete with battery that did transmit acceptable black and white images. But as the original measurements I had been given were 7cm square by 16cm deep, the camera didn't quite fit. One of the guy's present said that it didn't matter as we could strap the camera onto the front mount of the helicopter - and so that's what we did. I pushed the battery into the camera recess and then attached the camera to the front by elastic band, but I only had one.

The next day we were due to fly in a public park. To get there I was picked up from the hotel by a driver who gave me a carrier bag full of money that was my fee. To keep it from being pinched I stuffed it under the seat in the car. As we made our way to the park, the driver started to steer erratically. We would be going along when he would suddenly veer to the left. He would then accelerate and veer to the right. This happened a couple of times, which made me even more anxious. What I didn't know was that the driver thought we were being followed and wanted to lose the would-be stalker.

But it didn't work. A taxi pulled up alongside us and then another pulled in front of us and slammed on his brakes forcing the car I was in to stop. I was now terrified – what on earth had I gotten into? Were these people robbers after the money or was it something more sinister? I was told that the job was for the military and was secret but at no stage had I seen or had dealings with any military personnel. The man driving the car that had forced us to stop jumped out and ran to the door of the driver of my car. There he was man handled out onto the road and an argument ensued. It turned out that the drivers of the other taxis had thought my driver was drunk given his erratic steering. In Hungary, taxi drivers take it upon themselves to enforce the law and they had wanted to 'arrest' my driver for drunken driving. After a few loud exchanges and the smelling of breath, they decided to let my driver continue to the park. I was in no mood to fly!

On our arrival, I set up the model and once I was ready I was told to chase a dog in the park with the helicopter. With a little reticence I did as I was told and followed the dog – my contacts followed the chase eagerly on a screen that was picking up the pictures transmitted from the helicopter. I followed the dog around some bushes until it was out of site, which my sponsors thought was perfect. After a while I came back, landed and re-fuelled.

This time I was told to fly the helicopter to the top of a nearby building and look for a cross that was supposed to be up there. So I flew to the top of the building and with the aid of the camera found the cross. About this time I was getting hungry and asked if we could stop for lunch. I was told firmly that this wasn't possible and that we would eat in a few hours time. I tried arguing but it wasn't any good – I had to continue. "Right", I thought, "We'll see about that".

I took off and went looking for a 2nd cross which they asked me to find. They seemed quite interested as I identified its location but I had had enough of this. I was cold, hungry and needed a drink, and so I started to pump the pitch control so that the model started to bounce up and down. "What's wrong with it", asked my hosts. "It must be turbulence", I replied.   I carried on pumping the pitch control. "It's getting worse", I cried, "The turbulence is terrible."

By now I was making it sway left right, forwards, backward and shouting "I can't control it". I pulled away from the building I was flying over and placed the helicopter over the road. I then pumped the pitch control once to often and the elastic band broke, sending the camera, which was still sending pictures, followed by the battery hurtling to the ground. All I could hear my colleagues say was that mother earth was getting closer and closer and then the screen went black.

I was put into a car and taken back to the hotel without any food. We went past MacDonald's but the driver wouldn't stop. The person who had hired me came storming in and complained about the model – but I told him that he had given me stolen cameras. Our relationship was clearly at an end and I was put back into a car and taken to the airport. I never did find out what they were filming and in some ways I'm glad I didn't. I'll never go back there again as who knows what awaits me on entering the country. That was one of my bad trips.

Crossing the Channel

Crucial to the success of any business is keeping it in the mind of potential customers. For someone whose livelihood is based on radio control helicopters, it was important to keep my achievements in the press. I was having some success and that gave me some recognition. I was invited to fly at Wembley Stadium during the interval while they were filming the popular TV game show 'It's a Knockout', which gave me the opportunity to meet Bobby Charlton.

I was also invited to teach Wilson Fittipaldi, the brother of Indycar champion and F1 world champion Emerson Fittipaldi, to fly radio control helicopters. This took place over a three week period for which I was paid by cheque. I was so chuffed to have a cheque with the famous Fittipaldi name on it, that I never cashed it. It's still in my attic somewhere.

To keep my profile high meant that I had to keep doing stunts that captured the general public's imagination. I made an attempt on world speed record but failed when the helicopter crashed on its return run. And then came the opportunity of crossing the English channel.

In the UK, being the first to cross the channel, whether by swimming or flying, has always guaranteed press coverage. I had read in one of the modelling magazines that the model manufacturer Graupner had claimed to have crossed the channel with a radio-controlled helicopter but that it had been badly damaged on landing. On further investigation I found out that to gain the title 'first', the model still had to be flyable at the end of the challenge and because this wasn't the case with the Graupner attempt, the title was still available. So I decided that I would go for it.

In order to ensure press coverage I got in contact with Colin Cameron Tough, editor of the high quality 'International Helicopter' magazine. He agreed that they would not only cover the attempt in the magazine, but they would also supply the full-size helicopters needed. True to his word, Colin arranged for two Eurocopter AS355 Squirrel Helicopters – one would carry me from where I would fly the model and one from which photos could be taken of the attempt.

It took three months to design and build two models for the challenge. The biggest problem facing the design was to keep the model under 6kg in weight including fuel, as this was the limit placed by UK airspace regulations for radio control models. To help achieve this I made the mechanics out of titanium and magnesium, which then allowed a fuel payload of ¾ gallon. This amount of fuel was sufficient to get the model across the channel, provided I kept up a flying speed of around 45-60kph.

I had wanted to fly the model in both directions across the channel, but for some reason UK customs would not allow me to take off from England, so the attempt would only be one way – from Calais to Dover.

On my first attempt from Calais, I faced a head wind of around 30kph, which meant I had to

Above: Successfully crossing the English channel

Below: London Fire Brigade BK117 on display at a trade show

Above: Olive with Len's CH-47 Chinook
Below: Len with his super scale model of a Bell AH-1 Cobra

fly at speeds in excess of 80+kph. After half an hour of flying I was only achieving 16kph, so in conjunction with the pilot of the full size helicopter, we decided to abort the flight.

The second attempt happened a couple of months later. Again Colin agreed to cover the event and supply the aircraft, only this time I had the use of a Hughes 500, while he would be flying in a small aeroplane. The interior of the Hughes 500 had just been refitted at great expense and so it was vital that we kept it clean and without damage. To help me fly the model, the doors of the 500 were removed and left in the UK – a big mistake.

After arriving in Calais and getting prepared to take off, we heard that the weather in Dover had turned nasty and that it would be impossible to land at the planned location. Ten minutes later it started to rain where we were – right into the cabin of the Hughes 500, ruining the brand new interior. An hour later my daughter called from the UK to say that the weather there was now much better but would only last for a further hour. 15 minutes later, the weather in Calais improved, so we decided to make the attempt right away.

The trip was uneventful until we got 550 metres from the landing zone when I noticed that the tail rotor had stopped indicating that the engine had also stopped. To get the 'first' title, the rules stated that I had to land within 60 metres of pre-arranged landing spot, which meant that I had to auto rotate-glide the model for at least 500 metres. I was flying at around 240 metres in height, but I knew in my heart I knew that I wasn't going to make it. In front I could see a cornfield so I chose to stretch the glide for as far as I could and land in the field. Fortunately the sun had come out and so I could see the shadow of the model moving closer to the actual model, which helped me to judge how high it was above the ground. As the two met I put on collective pitch and hoped it was a soft landing. The observer who was monitoring the attempt said he wasn't sure that it had landed inside the required landing zone, so he was going to measure it. Fortunately it was just inside the limit by the small margin of 3 metres!

To get the title, all I had to do now was to make sure that the model wasn't damaged. With fear and trepidation I pulled it out of the corn. There was a small amount of fuel left in the tank (the clunk on the fuel pipe hadn't picked up all of the liquid due to the forward lean attitude of the model in flight). To my delight the engine started and I brought the model up into a steady hover. The title was mine.

Unfortunately Collin, who was supposed to have taken photos of the celebration, wasn't there. He had taken shots of us as we left Calais and had then jumped into his aeroplane to follow us. But by the time they were in the air, we had gone and they couldn't find us. Still, we did get some photos and a story in his magazine.

5: Travelling the World

Europe is a great place to travel but as it is still fairly close to home, it doesn't always feel that 'foreign'. However, with my helicopters I was invited to many far away places – places I would never had seen had it not been for this great hobby of mine.

New Zealand

In 1991 I was being sponsored by Gorham Model Products (GMP) of California that specialised in making radio control helicopters. My job was to go around promoting their products. One day John Gorham asked me if I would like to go on an all expenses paid trip to New Zealand to fly and conduct some seminars. As I was also selling my own manufactured rotor blades to a model shop in New Zealand at the time I jumped at the chance. However I don't like to speak at seminars because of a stutter, so we agreed that the format of these sessions would be that they would ask me a question and I would answer them. The only drawback was this was going to be over the Christmas holidays and I would be leaving Olive at home.

When I arrived in New Zealand I stayed in the house of the person who imported my blades into Auckland, who also happened to be a GMP importer. The deal was for me to travel down to Wellington to do the seminars - there must have been around 12 of them.

On the second day I was due to do some exhibition flights so in preparation I put one of the models together and had a test flight. As soon as I went into the hover the model started to pirouette – fast. It felt like something had come loose, and because I thought it would smash itself to pieces if I tried to land with it spinning, I did the next best thing and that was to open up the throttle.

Up went the model with it still pirouetting away like crazy. I could hear the guys behind me saying – "Cor, this guys good" – they had no idea the trouble I was in. Once I got high enough I decided to shut down the engine to try and stop the spinning, and to then attempt an auto landing. This worked a treat except I misjudged how far away the model was and I ended up landing in a tree.

It took about four hours with a rope and ladder to get up to it – there was no way I was going to climb the tree. We got it down and to our surprise nothing was broken. But what I did find was that the screw that held the control arm to the tail rotor bell crank had fallen out, which meant I had no control over the tail, hence the pirouetting. That taught me big lesson to always check the control surfaces before any flight. Something that I have always done since that day.

I put a new screw in and flew again that afternoon. I had been extremely lucky as the model could have easily fallen through the tree and onto the ground where it would have been badly damaged. New Zealand is a long way to go to only have had one test flight!

The rest of the trip went very well with flying demonstrations during the day and the seminar 'interviews' in the evening. Having done around seven sessions in the North Island, I arrived in Wellington. By this time it was very close to New Year, which also turned out to be the same time as their national championships.

As it was a holiday and I had nothing to do, I asked if I could enter the competition. I was told I couldn't as it was only for New Zealand modelling members. So I asked if I could join which wasn't a problem with them so I paid my membership fees, entered the FAI F3C competition and won it!

Although the organisers were quite happy that I had won, the bosses of their association were unhappy with me taking the trophy away. As they handed it to me they asked if I would return it at the end of the evening, as it wasn't to leave the country. I said this was no trouble at all.

While it was in my possession I met a few Maui's who were also modellers. I mentioned that I had to give the trophy back as it had to reside in New Zealand and that I would be going home in a few days. We parted company at the end of the evening and I thought nothing more about it.

The following morning I went to the club field and to my surprise the Maui's I had been with the previous evening were also there in all their regalia. They then presented me with a hand carved trophy identical to the one that I had been presented with the previous day. It even had my name on it and stating that I was the New Zealand national champion. Apparently they had stayed up all night carving the trophy for me. It's something I cherish. I haven't been back since but I'd love to go again.

Kuwait

I went on one trip with five other modellers to fly our models at a festival in Kuwait. This was being organised by Bob Davies, a 'brit' I knew, who ran a company there that manufactured target drones. I planned to take a pod and boom model as well as a scale Bell Huey model that I had built that was in US colours.   The organisers asked me if I would re-paint the Huey it in Kuwaiti colours – which I did and as a result I got a free trip.

All the models we were taking, which apart from my helicopters included spitfires, hurricanes and a Super 60 toffee bomber, went into two 4 metre long trailers that was to be loaded onto the aircraft. Unfortunately we had made the trailer too high by around 12cm so to get it on board we had to deflate the tyres. We all flew business class on Kuwait airlines, which was something that had to be seen to be believed.

On our arrival the trailer was confiscated by Kuwaiti customs officials (we never did find out why) and left out in the open. When we did get the trailers back some days later, all of the canopies in the models had sunk in where they had been melted by the heat of the sun and the wheels had gone flat. So we had to go to a local model shop to replace most of the damaged items.

The venue for the festival was a stadium and as the focus was on sport there was a variety of events on show including football, trampoline, track events and so on. Our slot was for 25 minutes and would be performed in front of the Shar of Kuwait. The organisers told me that I would be carrying two photographs of the Shar measuring 100cm x 80cm wide suspended from my scale Huey. This was in addition to the 'live' rockets that the model also carried. I could fire these while in the air where they would travel around 10 metre before exploding. I had 12 of these on each side of the helicopter.

I didn't think that all this weight would be a problem so I didn't practice. When my time came to fly it was very hot - around 90-95 degrees. There was a table with a gold cloth draped over it with my helicopter sitting on top. On each of the corners were four Kuwaitis in white robes, who had carried out the photo of the Shar. This was then attached to the helicopter by thin cat gut and hung down the side of the table away from the crowd so they couldn't see it. As I took off from the table, the Shar's photo then appeared to float up on its own from the gold cloth on the table. I then had to join the procession walking towards the Shar.

I was fortunate that the wind was coming from my right, which helped prevent the photo from rotating. Behind the group I was in were the four Kuwaitis carryng the gold cloth. My job was to fly the helicopter level with the Shar, face him, bow with the helicopter then rotate 180 degrees and fire the rockets, being very careful not to get the order wrong!

All went well until I reached the Shar and faced him. I was now downwind and as I bowed the wind got beneath the bottom of the rotor and immediately lost lift. The model started to fall and my heart was in my mouth. The last thing I wanted to do was to drag the Shars photo through the tarmac, sand and dirt. With some quick stick work I managed to keep it off the ground, turn 180 degrees and fire the rockets. Immediately a Zulu war chant erupted from the crowd that went around the stadium making the hairs on the back of my head go stiff as though they had been starched - and it hurt . The noise was horrifying – I had goose pimples on my arms and even the other guys who were walking with me said it was a frightening experience.

The procession continued and peeled off to go under a tunnel but as I couldn't go under due to the helicopter, the four Kuwaitis rushed by me with the gold cloth. Each one held a corner and I had to fly over the cloth while another one cut the strings holding the photo, all so that the photo didn't touch the dirt on the ground. That was one of the more unusual requests I've had.

India

I was asked many years ago if I would be willing to put on a show in Bombay – now called Mumbai – to help out the local aero modelling club.   As you've probably guessed by now I'll go anywhere as I enjoy flying and meeting other people. I asked a friend of mine– John Wallington – to come with me who also took one of his helicopters.

We arrived in Bombay airport and went through customs without any bother as our helicopters were in our suitcases. We had managed to dismantle them and fit them in with our clothes. However, this turned out to be a mistake as our contact – Darius Engineer – who was supposed to pick us up was looking for two people with helicopters. We had never met before and so neither of us knew what the other looked like. We were there for an hour and a half but no one approached us.   In the end, there were only three people left in the arrivals hall, John, myself and this other person. Plucking up courage I went up to him and asked if he was Darius – which he was. He said he hadn't spoken to us as he was expecting his people to be carrying large boxes containing the models rather than the suitcases we had!

Darius took us to our hotel, which turned out to be a really classy place. We reassembled our models in our room and were then taken by taxi to the club. This also wasn't a good idea as travelling by taxi seems like a sure way to die, as anyone who has travelled in India will tell you.

Arriving at the airfield, security appeared to be very strict even though this was just the practice day. We were told where the crowd would be and that we would be sharing the space with some Indian modellers flying their aeroplanes.   There would also be a full size flying display going on as well.

In order to promote the event I had to fly one of my models inside the 'Gateway of India' - a monumental arch in Mumbai located on the waterfront, which commemorated the visit of King George V and Queen Mary in December 1911. I believe I am still the only person who has been allowed to do this.

We couldn't wait for the day of the actual show, but when it came to our surprise there was nobody there. We were told by the organisers that the crowd would start coming within the hour, and that's what happened. First, just a trickle of people, and then more and more, until the queue for the entrance stretched as far as the eye could see. On the field itself, wherever you looked there were people behind barriers. We were told that there was a 30km tailback of traffic on the roads waiting to get into the airfield and that they had closed the gates as they couldn't fit anymore in. This must have been one of the largest crowds I have flown in front of.

I started off with my usual party trick – take off, go into a hover and then fly inverted 60cm above the ground. Then I'd do a couple of pirouettes and fly around. John said "The crowds quiet". Despite the number of people there, no one was saying a word. There was I doing low inverted passes, stall turns, wingovers, rolls – and yet there was no reaction from the crowd.

Then I did a loop and suddenly there was a 'uhh' from the crowd. So I did another one and again there was a 'uhh' from the crowd. So I thought ok. I asked Derius who was commentating to get the crowd to start counting the loops. So I started off and the crowd counted in English one, two, three ... Before long the crowd were yelling out the numbers ... nineteen, twenty, twenty-one ... they were really getting into it. As a finale I came across the flight line with a low inverted pass but the crowd went quiet, it was if they were bored. So I pulled up into another loop 'uhh' they responded. The only time I could get them to respond was in performing loops and fast climbing pirouettes! For the rest of the day, in the sessions where John and I flew, we just kept to loops, pirouettes and not much else.

During one of these sessions John said that he had a problem - the engine on his helicopter had cut out. I told him to do an autorotation the best he could, which he did, but it landed quite a long distance away. I said to John not to fetch it and that we'd collect it at the end of our session. When the session had ended, we looked down the line for John's helicopter but couldn't see it. Then we noticed it being carried over the heads of the crowd – hand over hand, from one person to the next – all the way down the line. It must have gone for at least 500 metres all the way to us and there wasn't a mark on it. Unbelievable.

During another one of the sessions where I was flying, I noticed a young Indian girl in the VIP enclosure, so I asked Darius to go and ask her if she would like to fly my helicopter. The idea was that the girl would take hold of John's transmitter (which wasn't flying anything) and I would be hidden among the other pilots controlling the helicopter that she would be 'flying'.

The girl was willing to do this so John gave her his transmitter and was telling her what to do over the loudspeaker system. Meanwhile I was actually flying the model, hidden from the crowd so no one would notice. I started off with some gentle hovering and careful, slow circuits. Then the commentator said "how about a loop and roll". So the girl starts twiddling the sticks and off goes the helicopter into a loop and a roll. Still the crowd had no idea that it was me flying the helicopter. The crowd went wild as she 'performed' each manoeuvre. At the end of the flight, she got a standing ovation - the crowd never did find out.

That was fun. I still keep in contact with Darius.

6: Tagging Whales in the Arctic

I've done many things with my helicopters, ranging from crossing the English channel, through to spying missions in Eastern Europe. But perhaps the strangest and yet the most challenging took place in the Arctic.

Background

I was in Essex with a colleague of mine, practicing for the team trials for the European F3C championships. We were in a very large playing field that consisted of 15 football grounds. It was so large that to get to where we were flying we had to drive around the edge of the field. While practicing I noticed a car coming towards me right across the field rather than going around it. It was a taxi that pulled in front of me while I was still flying. A man with a beard got out and said "Hey man, do you reckon that you can land that thing on the back of a whale?"

As I was focused on practicing for the competition, which he had rudely interrupted, I told him to "sod off". Then added "If you want to speak to anyone then go to the guys standing behind me." With that he cleared off, the taxi moved and I finished off my tank of fuel. Afterwards I went up to him and said "What right do you have to drive right across this playing field – we have to drive around it?"

"Ah well", he said, "I work in that university on the edge of the field." "Oh", I said, "What do you do?" He said that he studied whales and other sea creatures on behalf of an oil company and that he was trying to find out the migration route of whales from Alaska to California. This was because the company was planning to drill for oil and they didn't want to interfere with their migration path.

I asked him what he wanted me to do and he explained his situation. They wanted to put radio beacons onto the whales so they could plot the route they took around the Arctic, but placing them on the back of the whale was proving to be very difficult. They had tried by firing them from a crossbow with a hook that would attach itself to the whale but nine times out of ten the crossbow would hit the whale below its natural waterline, which meant they couldn't pick up the signal being transmitted.

He went on to say that while sitting in his office he had seen me flying and thought that it would great if he could use a radio control helicopter, as full size helicopters tend to scare the whales under water. He wondered if it would be possible for a model helicopter to land right on the back of a whale and place the radio beacon so that it would be above water for most of the time. He had come out to ask if it could be done and how much it would cost.

I thought it was possible but as for the cost he would have to ask someone else. There was a

53

model shop owner near to where I was flying so I sent him to speak to them. I was intrigued so while I was fuelling up for my next flight I tried to eaves drop on the conversation. I could hear them talking telephone numbers for costs, it sounded like he was going to be charged an absolute fortune. I had another round of practice and when I finished I went up to the guy and said that I knew what he was going to be charged but that if he wanted to rent my helicopters then I was interested. I gave him my card and told him to bugger off.

As he left he said "I bet you couldn't hit the roof of this taxi before I get out of this field". He hadn't got more than 100 metres from me before I hit the taxi three times. That evening I got a phone call from him. He said he was very interested in renting my helicopters. I asked him where we would be going. I was amazed when he said Prudhoe Bay in Alaska.

Preparation

I didn't do any homework for the trip other than prepare two helicopters that would carry the radio beacon hanging from the helicopter body. I widened the undercarriage to accommodate this and as it was going to be over water I fitted it with floats so that I could land on water. My back garden pond proved that this would work fine.

The radio beacon they wanted to place on the whales were expensive – around $45,000 each and so we had to make sure that each one counted. The beacon itself was square and had ten needles on each side. A pressure sensor on the device would fire these needles at an angle into the skin of the whale provided it was placed down firmly. Each needle contained antibiotics that would prevent any wounds from becoming infectious. After around three months the needles would decay and fall out, thereby releasing the tag. During this time the tag would be transmitting the whale's location.

To make sure the beacon attached properly, I would have to land quite firmly, but squarely on the whale's back. If I hit the whale without enough pressure the beacon would fall off when the whale went under water and we would lose it. To prevent this happening I suggested that a wire was fitted to each beacon that was also attached to the helicopter. If the beacon didn't attach properly, the helicopter would be able to pull it off, allowing us to re-use it later on. If the beacon did attach properly then I would release the cable from the helicopter where it would be free to stay with the whale.

Trouble with Customs

The date to leave soon came and I jumped on a plane to Anchorage in Alaska. To transport the helicopters I took them apart and packed them into two suitcases that were lined with 5mm plywood to protect them. The guy I was to meet – Bruce – would be waiting for me outside the terminal. But as I was leaving the terminal, I was stopped by customs officials who asked me what was in the suitcases.

I said that it was two model helicopters but they didn't seem to believe me and wanted to take a closer look. I took out the parts of the helicopter and showed them how it fitted together, which seemed to fascinate them. They then asked me where I was staying. When I said Prudhoe Bay they became suspicious again telling me that, "No one goes there – what are you going there for?"

I knew I couldn't say work, as I hadn't got a green card so I said it was for a holiday. "No, no", they said, "No one goes to Prudhoe Bay, least of all to have a holiday. Where are you staying?" I said that I was told it was going to be on a fishing boat. Well that did it, they told me there was something wrong with my story and so they took me away into for further interrogation. As they started the interview I said that to get the story straight, they needed to speak to the person I was meeting. The only trouble was that I didn't know his second name but I did know that his first name was Bruce, he had a beard and should be waiting for me the other side of customs. However they wouldn't check. After about an hour they made me pack my suitcases, as they couldn't find anything wrong. They ushered me out of customs and pointed to two men in white coats who were standing in a corner. They told me not to go anywhere near them or "... they'll take you away", making out that I was mentally unstable!

Delays

I finally went out and met Bruce in the arrivals hall who told me that we had a problem. We were due to get a connecting flight to Prudhoe Bay but there was a problem with the Eskimos. It was the start of the hunting season for them and they hadn't yet killed their sacrilegious whale. Without having done this they would not allow any 'outsiders' to go after them. The reason why they hadn't yet caught a whale was to do with the sea that was still frozen, which had pushed the whales out beyond the reach of their boats. The only thing we could do was to wait in Anchorage for three days or until we were allowed to travel to the bay.

It seemed pointless hanging around doing nothing, so I looked at a way of getting some practice on the task that faced me. There was a river a few miles away that had large chunks of ice floating on it. I thought I could use these as practice for landing on whales and so that's what I did. I would take off from the shore, fly over the mini icebergs and try and land on them as they floated by. After two days I was pretty good at it, but then the police arrived and asked me to stop flying. Evidently I was attracting quite a crowd who came to watch me and their cars were blocking the road so that no one could get through.

On the third day we were told we could fly to Prudhoe Bay, and so we went back to the airport and got into the flimsiest aircraft I have ever been in. This thing shakes. As we took off all the lockers opened because of the shaking and I started to wonder if we were ever going to make it. But make it we did and we landed at Prudhoe Bay some two hours later.

It was then I started to regret that I hadn't done any research. It was cold – far colder than could be handled by any of the clothes I had bought. However, Bruce managed to get hold of some suitable clothing for me – boots, gloves and a survival suit. The first night as I was lying in bed, I was excited about being in such a wild, but beautiful environment. It was 10:30pm but the evening was about to get even better. We couldn't get onto the fishing boat as the ice was still bad so we stayed at a hut that was quite comfortable. Bruce told me not to go to sleep as we were going to go out later that night. I said that I was dog-tired and wanted to stay in bed but he told me I couldn't.

About 12 midnight there was a knock on my door and I'm told to grab a blanket, a pillow and to come outside. I was still fully dressed and so half asleep I followed Bruce's instructions. There were already quite a few people there with their blankets and pillows laying on the ice. I thought – what on earth were they doing, what were they waiting for? I soon had the answer. As I lay down I could hear crackling noises in the atmosphere followed by a flash of red and green lights that criss-crossed the sky. It was the Northern lights, or to give them their correct name, the aurora borealis. Lights flashed from the right and went over to the left. Different colours all accompanied by whining and cracking noises. It was spectacular - words fail to describe what it was like. One thing was for sure, it was well worth staying up.

The following morning we still couldn't go out as the Eskimos hadn't killed their whale, so we decided to do some more practicing. I was told that I would have to fly for at least a minimum of one hour. As a standard flight typically only lasts 15 minutes, I had to do something with the fuel tanks. I went to the cookhouse and found some large bottles that fitted perfectly in the back of the helicopter but this put the Centre of Gravity too far to back and would make the model un-flyable.

I managed to counteract this by adding extra weight to the front, extending the canopy and moving the battery and receiver tray forward. The new bottles allowed me to carry about 2 litres of fuel. To find out how long this would last I had to fly around until the fuel ran out. It was around minus 15C and after flying for a while I said to Bruce that I couldn't go for much longer than an hour. This was not only the limit for me just standing still and keeping my concentration, but it was also the limit for the batteries.

Bruce said that one hour shouldn't be a problem. I landed, refuelled, changed the batteries and took off again. But it wasn't too long before I started to get really cold. I was wearing gloves so they brought out two women from the cookhouse to aid me. One woman would wear a pair of my gloves, so that as my hands became cold I could swap them with the gloves being worn by the woman which were warm. She would then wear my cold gloves to warm them up again. We could do this as I flew with a transmitter tray, which meant I could take one hand off and still keep the model flying why they changed the gloves. The other women stayed behind me rubbing my legs (yes it was just my legs) to keep them warm. This meant we could satisfy everyone with the amount of time I could keep flying.

Landing on Icebergs

As part of our preparation we practiced flying the model helicopter from the full-size helicopter while in flight. This was exciting as it involved me wearing a full survival suit, sitting at the door entrance, feet out, flying my model. To stop the model being affected from the downwash of the full-size helicopter, I would place the model 100 metres in front. The model would take off first, followed by the full size. I would then try and keep the model at least 100 metres in front with the full-size helicopter following. This meant I had to be given instructions on where to go by the pilot who spoke to me via the helicopter intercom.

We also practiced landing on an iceberg. On the one we had chosen I noticed it had a signpost to many cities – Moscow, London, New York, Melbourne and so on. I wondered just how many cars would have seen that one! After we had landed I took out my model and fuelled it up. I sat back in the full-size helicopter and put the model into a hover as agreed. The pilot then said that he would take off into wind which meant banking the helicopter 180 degrees away from the model so I wouldn't be able to see it. This meant I had to increase the height of the model at the same time to make sure I could see it. However the pilot turned too fast and I lost sight of the model which made it quite thrilling.

Landing on icebergs, it turns out, is quite dangerous and landing on 'any old' berg was right out of the question. The reason was that we wouldn't know how stable it would be with the weight of helicopter and it could easily turn over pitching both the helicopter and ourselves into the water. The survival rate once in the water was only a matter of minutes due to the cold or polar bears that saw us as a tasty snack. We would be too far away to be rescued in time and so the pilot would only land on those that were large and known to be able to take the weight. Because of this I had an agreement with the helicopter pilot that if the model went down, it stayed down. We would not rescue it for any reason. Bruce had insurance that would cover any damages or losses to the model helicopter.

However, on the way back from one of these training flights, I could see that the white tail blades on the model were doing a 'V for Victory' sign at me, which meant that the engine had stopped. Losing the model at this early stage of the engagement would be a disaster as there was no hope of visiting a local model shop to get another one. I did have a backup model but this was for when we started the tagging operation as we were bound to lose one in doing this.

I said to Bruce that I had an engine problem and that I needed to auto-rotate otherwise I would loose control on landing. The model started to descend sharply as there was no engine power, but the pilot wasn't able to keep up with the speed of descent. The model was getting smaller and smaller as it raced towards the surface of an iceberg. I knew that I was going to have to put on full pitch when it was near to the ground, but I daren't do it too late as the model would hit the ground far too fast to make any kind of recovery worthwhile, and if I did it too early the model would stall and still crash.

Fortunately it was a lovely sunny day so I knew I could look out for the model's shadow on the ground to give me an indication of when it was getting near to the surface of the iceberg. When the model and the shadow got close together I put on full pitch but I miss-timed it. It was too high and I could see the speed of the rotor disc decaying, so I put in negative pitch to wind it up again. I was probably still around 150 metres above the model but I looked for the shadow and the model getting closer together for a second time. This time I got it right and the model landed perfectly ok.

I said to Brice that it was in one piece, to which he replied 'Great - let's go down and pick it up". The pilot disagreed and reminded us our agreement of not to rescue any 'downed' models. I said that if he could hover or just touch down lightly while still keeping the power on in the middle of the iceberg, then at least we could jump off and attempt getting it back. He agreed to this so I sat with my legs out of the door on the right side of the helicopter, while Bruce did the same on the left. The pilot manoeuvred the helicopter over a pinnacle on the iceberg and as Bruce was eager to retrieve the helicopter, he jumped out before I did. Immediately the helicopter started to tip backwards as it was now unbalanced. I jumped out and my helper on board the helicopter shouts out that I wasn't to move backwards towards the tail or I would get 'a mouthful of tail-blades'.

On seeing the danger I rushed around to the front as the helicopter takes off. The downdraft of the blades now pushes me onto my back on the ice and start sliding towards the front of the iceberg where it sits in the water. I have my radio transmitter in one hand and I dig it into the ice to stop myself being blown off the edge. I turned myself over and dug for all my worth and managed to stop about one foot away from the water. To my amazement I saw Bruce 'walking on water' towards the model. It turned out the water was only an inch or so deep and underneath it was ice, so he was able to retrieve the model.

We got hold of the model, folded back the blades and started to look around for the helicopter. We also looked out for polar bears as we knew they were in the area and here we were completely unarmed. After what seemed to be an age, the helicopter came back but would only land on the same ridge and in the same way as last time. Once the pilot had touched the ice, Bruce got in which caused the helicopter to start sliding off the pinnacle. The pilot seeing the danger did an immediate take-off and I was left on the iceberg completely alone. I was now really worried because if a polar bear does come along all I've got is a model helicopter to throw at him.

The full-size helicopter came in for a second time. I threw in the model to my helper and I got one foot onto the float, lifted myself up to grab my safety harness with one hand, and tried to slam the door with my other hand. Straight away the pilot lifted off and banked the helicopter in my direction. I'm now hanging on for dear life to the safety harness and trying to get the door shut.

Above: Alongside the whale spotter plane
Below: Practicing before heading north

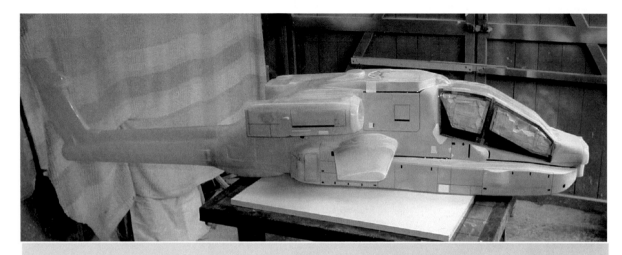

Len's Apache bristles with scale detail, particularly in the weapons department. Everything except for turbine and radio was built from scrap materials.

Once the pilot had levelled out we managed to close the door and off we flew. The pilot asked us not to mention the incident when we got back as he could lose his license. But it was so exciting. In bed that night I shook so much because of the fear of what we had been through, that the bed vibrated.

Tagging Whales

After a few days of preparation we were told that the Eskimos had killed their whale, so we were allowed to go ahead with our job. An Otter spotter airplane would be looking for the whales, while I would be in a full size Bell Longranger helicopter that would be sitting on the water. Once a whale had been spotted, I would place my model helicopter on the water beside the full size helicopter and we would then both take off in tandem with me controlling the model from the full-size helicopter. We would fly together to the whale as directed by the spotter plane and as we closed in I would fly the model over the top of the whale and place the radio beacon that was attached to the model.

Well that was the plan, but unfortunately every time we got close to a whale it would disappear under water having been scared off by the noise of the full size helicopter. We tried five different helicopters including a Jet Ranger, Bell 212, and a B0105 – but they were all too noisy which was a big problem. To overcome this we took a 2 metre rubber dingy in the back of the helicopter out to a large iceberg, which Bruce and I would then use as a base to chase the whales. Bruce would be at the back of the dinghy with a walky-talky in communication with spotter plane while I'm up front with my helicopter and starting equipment. When the plane spotted a whale they would radio Bruce and I would then put my model in the water, take off and we'd go after it.

This was working quite well until one time when I placed the beacon on the back of a whale I wasn't able to release the cable from the helicopter. The release mechanism was operated from a switch on my transmitter but on this occasion I had fitted a cover to the transmitter tray to protect my hands from the cold, and hadn't realised that it stopped me getting to the release switch. So there I was with my helicopter attached to a whale via the beacon cable that I couldn't release. It was like the whale was flying my helicopter like a kite. I struggled with my gloves while still trying to fly and eventually managed to take them off and squeeze my fingers between the transmitter and the cover. When I hit the release switch there was a loud 'boinngg' sound as the helicopter catapulted off the line. Fortunately I managed to recover flight and we removed the transmitter cover!

As I said at the start of this chapter, this trip was one of the most exciting I had been on. There was talk about a further engagement, but unfortunately, nothing came of it. I found out later that another model helicopter pilot had learned of what we had done and because I didn't have a green card and that any US job must first be offered to a US citizen, he stepped in and claimed the job for his son.

7: Competitions

There's nothing like competition to hone both your building and flying skills but for me it's something far more. It is the major driving force that takes me on to set new standards of craftsmanship. I don't enter competitions to come second – I enter them to win.

Apart from the buzz you get from winning against your peers, competition has also bought me other benefits. The most obvious is fame that helped my business to grow, but probably best of all are the friendships I've built up with other competitors, many of which have lasted the test of time.

In the past I used to go to the World and European championships, but you only meet those attending every other year so there is little chance to build up a relationship. Now I tend to go to events where I get to meet a bunch of guys on a regular basis, many of whom are great company and have become very good friends.

Overcoming nerves

It took me quite a while to enjoy competing. My first competitions were mainly 'fun' events that tested the skill of pilots. They typically ran along the lines of knocking over bottles or bursting balloons with the undercarriage, but there was nothing serious.

For me they were anything but fun. I was a shy guy who stuttered quite a bit and so I tried to avoid any kind of publicity. To make matters worse, as soon as I took off in front of any kind of crowd, I would become very nervous. My arms would shake, my legs would shake and the hairs on the back of my neck would stand on end so much that it hurt. And so it would continue for the duration of any flight made in front of an audience. To try and calm my nerves I would chain smoke. Things were so bad that my helper would light up my cigarettes and stick them in my mouth while I was flying.

I can remember going with my wife Olive to a 'fun fly' event on the south coast which took us several hours to get to. I had a bright orange Cobra that looked fantastic, but it stayed in the car, as I was just too shy to bring it out. On the way home I knew I could have won the event, so I resolved there and then to get over my fear of crowds.

Then one day a friend of mine came up to me after a flight and said "Put your model on the floor and look behind you". I did as he said and turned around to see a large crowd of people looking at me – they actually wanted to see me. The very thought should have frightened me but for some reason it didn't. Something changed within me that day. As I saw them looking I thought to myself "I can't let them down because I'm the only person flying". That broke the ice. Although I still get nervous in competitions – after all if you don't get a buzz when flying then why on earth are you doing it – it wasn't as nerve racking as it had been.

Since then I have flown in over 800 competitions – many of them at a national level. In that time I have won 21 national championships (five of which were in one year), over 250 other championships and was rarely out of a top three placing in the others. To begin with I competed in aerobatic competitions but in my later years I swapped to scale as for me, this is where you can really 'wow' the general public. It's also a lot cheaper!

World aerobatic championships

I've flown in four F3C world championships. My first championship was in London Ontario, Canada in 1985, which, as it turned out, was also the first world championship for RC Helicopters. These were being organized by the Federation Aeronautique Internationale, otherwise known as the FAI, based in Switzerland. They organize the world championships for a range of model aircraft disciplines and with the increasing popularity of helicopters and their ability to do more than just 'hover', the time was right to introduce a competition that would show what could really be achieved. The FAI F3C schedule was to consist of a range of complex hovering manouvres as well as aerobatic shapes that would test both the pilot and the model.

This first championship attracted a lot of interest, with 37 participants from 17 countries. At that time I was flying my own model based on heavily modified Schluter mechanics and my own design and manufactured body kit, which had given me a lot of success, including qualifying for the three-man UK team. In the lead up to the event, I was contacted, out of the blue, by Walt Schoonard, who was the US importer of Schluter kits. He wanted me to come and help them develop accessories for those kits, but who would also release me to fly in the upcoming championships.

Walt wanted me to go to the US for three months, initially to Florida where he lived, so I could start working for him. The plan was that he would get me my green card in that time, and then he would bring Olive across towards the end of the three months. Olive and I could then look around for a suitable house and settle down out there. This looked like an opportunity to good to miss, so I moved to the US leaving Olive behind in the UK, but in anticipation of her moving out soon to be with me.

On arriving at my new employer's factory I started to unpack my models that I had sent out by cargo ship a few weeks earlier. Straight away he asked me what I was doing. He told me that I couldn't use my modified machines but only the standard Schluter machines – he then confiscated my competition models.

This didn't go down too well with me but as I had very little money and that he had bought me out on a one-way ticket, there wasn't much I could do about it. I ended up flying a standard kit with a standard engine using 30% nitro instead of the 5% I was used to. I'm not a nitro person. I would far sooner get more power out of an engine through a tuned exhaust pipe.

After a few weeks preparation we drove from Florida to Ontario, Canada for the world championships. It was a very long way in my employer's motor home. On arriving, I stayed in a dormitory of a local college that was close to where the event was being held. My roommate was John Wallington who was (and still is) a good friend of mine who knew something was wrong with me. I was frustrated that I wasn't able to configure or change the model to suit my style of flying. One of the problems was the engine. I had been supplied with an Enya which my sponsor made me use with a high nitro content fuel. However, John had a spare engine – a Webra – complete with a tuned exhaust pipe – the same that I was used to using. So I swapped out my engine for his and after three days of practice I was getting back to my normal self.

I'm proud to say that at the very first world championships I won the first round! I was numbed by what I had achieved. Although I had practiced a lot before setting off for America, the past three months had been bad given that I wasn't flying a model that I was used to. I also gained a perfect score (five 10s') for my auto rotation, which I believe I'm still the only person to have ever gained a perfect five man score.

On the second round I dropped from first to third place as my engine was giving me grief and I didn't have a spare. The engine problems continued and I ended up with a final placing of either 4th or 5th for which I was very, very pleased with. On reflection I don't think I could have won, even with my own models, as the manoeuvres I chose – loops and rolls - did not have the highest K factors. The people who finished ahead of me had chosen far more difficult manoeuvres, which the points system favoured. It was a Japanese guy who won – a very good flier – who defiantly deserved to win.

After the championship the plan was to work for my sponsor developing new designs for helicopter models, along side his son. But right away the relationship seemed to have soured. Maybe it was because I didn't win or perhaps because I had beaten his son in the competition. I was well liked by the other competitors, which also seemed to go against me. What finally finished it was on the way home I mentioned that I was looking forward to getting back to his place and seeing Olive, who was due to fly out and be with me.

"Oh", replied my sponsor, "didn't I tell you - she's not coming". That was when I realised I had been stitched up. I had gone to America thinking that the three months I would be there would be really great, but it turned out to be the worst three months of my whole modelling career.

I did three other F3C world championships – every other year – in Finland, Austria and Switzerland. In each competition I finished in the top 10, but for me that wasn't good enough. I remember on one occasion while in America, I was having a bad day and couldn't sort my model out. It was late afternoon but already dark outside and as my hotel room was big enough I thought I would check out the helicopter by hovering it there. I cleared the room by putting anything that could get blown around into the bathroom including the bed mattress, and shut all the windows. I then placed the model on the frame of the bed and started it up. The only problem was that the under carriage kept getting caught up in the bed springs, so I decided to put the mattress back on top of the bed and fly off of this. Big mistake.

I took off and forgot about the oil residue that comes out of the exhaust pipe. When I had finished flying you couldn't see anything in the room due to the exhaust smoke so I opened up the windows to clear the air and saw a large, black oil stain on the mattress. I couldn't put the clean sheets back on this so I turned the mattress over with the oil stain now facing downwards onto the bed springs and left it at that. I didn't get a complaint from anyone about the noise as it was only 8pm in the evening so most people were probably at dinner. I never did hear back from the hotel about the bed.

Scale Competitions

As I mentioned in chapter three, between 1977 and 1997 I won 15 national aerobatic championships and although competition at this level wasn't boring but it did get repetitious. To keep winning I had to practice on a regular basis and in all weathers. A typical week would consist of flying for around 2 – 3 hours each day from Monday through to Friday, helping fellow flyers on a Saturday with Sunday being reserved for producing blades and building models.

This was very expensive in terms of both time and money. I was getting through eight gallons of fuel each week, which at £12 a gallon equated to around £6,000 per annum on fuel alone. In addition to this I would get through five, 'top of the range' 60 size engines, although one year I managed to destroy eleven. At this level, flying aerobatic helicopters isn't a cheap hobby and is unsustainable unless you are sponsored full-time.

As I got older my reactions were getting slower so I had to practice even harder. Then one day I decided I had had enough and so I went back into scale modelling.

US Top Gun: Jet Engines

One of the first international competitions I entered in this new era of scale modelling was the Top Gun show in the US. This show is among the top scale meetings held anywhere in the world. To be invited to fly at Top Gun is the ultimate accolade for any scale modeller and so when I was invited to the 2001 show, I jumped at the chance.

It came through David Sweatt of Dallas, Texas, who at that time I didn't know. David had evidently followed my progress through the modelling magazines and when he was asked by the Top Gun organizers to arrange a helicopter competition to go alongside the model aircraft for which the show was famous, he got in contact. For this first year the helicopter competition would be for static models only as no flying was being allowed, however they still had to be capable of flight if required. I wanted to build something special so I settled on the Aerospatiale N4 Dauphin, which no one had modelled before.

What made this helicopter 'special' was the fenstrom tail (where the tail blades are completely enclosed), which makes the model look exciting in the air but quite expensive for a kit manufacturer to produce. Having settled on the Dauphine N2 as used by the US Coastguard, I started researching the full size aircraft. This brought me in contact with the helicopter operator McAlpine who had one, however they suggested that I build the N4 version as it had only just come onto the market.

The model took me around five months to build. It had 26 opening panels, fully working lights and adjustable front seats. It certainly wowed the crowds at Top Gun but I had overlooked one crucial area of the competition. I should have provided a three-view diagram and paint samples of the full size machine so that the judges could see how accurate the model had been built. I knew it was accurate but I couldn't prove it, which lost me points. Once the judging of all models was complete I found out that I had missed first place by two-tenths of a point – giving me the nickname of Lenny two tenths. If only I had taken along the three-view drawings ….

For the remainder of my time at Top Gun I watched the aeroplanes fly. There was a great variety of power plants including two-stroke glo motors, four-stroke petrol engines and ducted fans. I then saw a jet with a turbine engine. The noise it made as it took off and flew past me was magic – just like the real thing. I said to my mate standing next to me that it would be absolutely fantastic to have that in a helicopter.

As soon as I had finished saying it, there was a tap on my shoulder and the person standing behind me said "What did you say?" I repeated that I would love to have one of those engines in one of my helicopters. He then asked me if I knew who he was. I said "No" to which he replied that he was the boss of RAM, who at that time made turbine engines for model jet planes.

We spoke some more over lunch and he agreed that we should get together to produce something to go into a helicopter. I mentioned that in a helicopter we didn't want thrust as required by aircraft, but instead we needed torque.

As we were talking it dawned on me that this would make an ideal entry to next years' Top Gun competition. As far as I was aware, no one else had ever attempted this so it would certainly have the 'wow' factor as well as being a 'bit of a challenge'. All I needed now was to decide what helicopter it would go into.

At that time I liked war films particularly from the Vietnam era, and the Bell Huey is an iconic helicopter of this age. The only kits on the market were for quite small models so I thought that building a larger version with a turbine engine would be a definite winner. Before I left, it was agreed that I would work on designing the model and mechanics, while RAM would work on a turbine combination that would suit a helicopter.

Well six months went by and I had heard nothing from RAM so I sent them a letter asking them what the situation was. They sent me back some very rough drawings which made me think that if this is all they had done in six months, then it was absolutely pointless and I was wasting my time. What a shame. That night a friend of mine in Germany phoned me up. During the conversation he said that I sounded a bit down and asked me what the trouble was. I explained the situation and said I was disappointed that I wouldn't be able to use a turbine at the next Top Gun event.

"Ah," he said, "you need to speak to Peter Jackadofsky". I had never heard of him, so I asked for his phone number and called him up. He told me that he had a turbine that would do the job but that he didn't have any mechanics. I said that it wasn't a problem as I could design a set of mechanics. Peter told me to send him the drawings and he would get them made. So I shipped him some rough drawings and a couple of weeks later he asked if he could come and visit me at my house in the UK. I said that was fine, so he came with the mechanics I had designed, fitted with a turbine engine that had an integrated gearbox. I had already built the Huey so all we had to do was to fit the mechanics.   With a little bit of effort the whole unit just slotted into place.

Peter was staying at a local hotel so the following day we went out to fly the jet powered Huey. By the end of the week we had it flying really well. It was a thrill and thankfully, quite uneventful. We didn't have any thrust problems from the engine as this was being destroyed by the downwash from the rotor blades. The blades I had made were big measuring 11cm wide by 120m long which produced the classic 'phwap, phwap, phwap' noise as the blades whipped round, just the same as you would hear on the full size.

After a few days, Peter went back home and left me with the turbine and mechanics. I now had to get the model ready for the Top Gun competition, which was only three months away. To make things more challenging I decided to keep the model I had as a test bed and build a brand new one from the moulds I had made.

I know I can build fast but my speed even surprised me. I managed to get the new model completed about three weeks before the competition. The model was a 'stunner' at over 2 metres long and weighing around 10 Kgs. It looked totally realistic both on the ground and in the air. It had a see-through cockpit from which no sign of the mechanics or engine could be seen. It was fitted with rockets that actually fired while in flight. Nothing can stop me from winning now – or so I thought.

With just a couple of weeks to go I received a letter from the Top Gun organisers asking me to supply a pilot profile which should also include details of the model I was planning to fly. This was to cover radio, servos and the engine I would be used. I was so chuffed at what we had achieved that I was really excited at putting on the form that the engine was a

PJW Jackadofsky turbine. As it turned out this was to be our downfall – I should never have mentioned that the engine was a turbine.

A week before the competition I received another letter saying that the Top Gun organisers were very sorry but that I couldn't enter the turbine I had stated. The reason was that the turbine hadn't been built, tested or manufactured in the US. This meant that all 'foreign' turbines were excluded.

There was no time to take the turbine out and put in petrol driven mechanics. However as I had already bought my flight tickets I still decided to go with Olive, but we would go as spectators instead and have a holiday.

Although I didn't take the model, I did take the turbine and mechanics. To our surprise there was so much interest in what we had achieved that we sold quite a few there and then. I later found out that there was one person who had prevented me flying, that had caused all the fuss around the 'foreign' turbine. The organisers were going to let me fly but this one person didn't want me to be the first person to fly a turbine-powered helicopter in the USA.

Unfortunately, there never was to be a turbine helicopter at Top Gun as the organisers decided to ban helicopters from all future competitions.

For me, turbines are the way to go. They look and sound great and you can have fun with them. In the very early days of using turbines, people would often come to my hotel room to see the model and as a party trick I would start it up for them. Of course I couldn't let it run up to full power so I would let it get to around 30,000 rpm and then shut the turbine down. The only thing is that after doing this a few times, fuel would collect in the turbine, which could easily ignite on a subsequent run, resulting in a spectacular flame over 1 metre long to exit from the exhaust pipe. And that is what happened on one occasion, which then set off the hotel room sprinklers and soaked everything. I had to be moved to another room but none of the hotel staff knew the reason why they had gone off in the first place.

US Nationals

The first US National scale competition I entered was in 1985 where I came 2nd, but rather than celebrate I was a bit upset as I thought I should have won. The competition was due to be held over five rounds and after the fourth round I was lying in 2nd place just one point behind the leader. I thought I was in with a good chance of winning, as I knew I could fly better and should be able to beat him on the last round, which was due to take place the following day.

I had a good nights sleep and arrived at the competition field early. I started to put my model together when the contest director came up to me and asked what I was doing. I told him I was getting my model prepared so I could take it easy leading up to the flight. "Oh", said the director, "Hasn't anybody told you – the flight has been cancelled."

Len's magnificent Dauphin N4 - best Interior winner and second overall (by 2 tenths of a point!) at the prestigious Top Gun event in the US

Above: Westland Lynx

Below: Cockpit detail from Len's Apache

"What do you mean it's been cancelled?", I replied with some surprise. "It's too windy", he came back at me. I couldn't believe it. To be quote honest I could fart faster than the wind was blowing – it couldn't have been more than 7kph. "When did you decide this? ", I asked. "Last night", he replied.

"How could you decide last night that today would be too windy", I protested, " and who decided that?" "Oh we had a pilots meeting at a hotel", he said. It turned out to be the same hotel I was staying at. I asked him why I hadn't been invited to which he replied that they couldn't find me.

So that was it. The last round had been cancelled and the championship decided after four rounds. Something didn't feel right but I guess that's the way that some championships are run. It left a sour taste in my mouth and I decided not to compete in the US again.

However, in 2006 I was invited back to compete in the US Nationals by Peter Wales, someone who I had known for some time. Peter had just taken over as contest director for the scale competition with a remit to build up the number of people competing. I was flattered to be asked but the problem was that the competition was only three months away and I didn't have a model. I told Peter about my situation to which he retorted, "Well get your finger out - you've got three months to build one!"

Peter knew my reputation as a fast builder so I thought OK, I'll give it a go. I don't like to build the same model twice, so my Huey, Cobra and Kiowa helicopters were out. Olive said to me, "Why don't you do the Westland Scout?" This was a model I had considered building a few years earlier but had given up. I had all the three-view drawings in my attic and thought this is it – let's get the plans blown up to the full size I need. So from a 15cm drawing I created a mould and built the scout in its military colours in just three months. Well I say built – what I had was a basic model ready to fly but without too much scale detail. And that's how it travelled to the US.

Normally I would test fly my models for several months before a competition but on this occasion I didn't have time. I had hoped to have a test flight before getting on the plane but illness had stopped me going out and I was seriously considering pulling out. But I had a sponsor and I didn't want to let them down so I planned to get there a day early so I could fly it just before the competition. But when I arrived at the site I found I wasn't allowed to fly, which meant the only time I could test fly it was during the first round. And so that is exactly what I did.

In that first round the other competitors looked with interest as it took off and flew around on its maiden flight. I wonder what they would have thought if they knew that this was also the first time I had seen it fly. However the flight wasn't the fairy tale I had been hoping for. The tail of the model was extremely lively and I struggled to keep it pointing in one direction as per the full size model. The problem was caused by the tail rotor, which was around 45cm in diameter. The slightest change in pitch resulted in a sharp, unwieldy movement. It seemed that the gyro couldn't hold a constant direction – I later found out it wasn't the gyro that was the problem but the servo I had fitted wasn't strong enough to cope with the loads.

Fortunately the first round involved two to four minutes of free-style, so I chose the manoeuvres that best suited the model in this condition and that would also allow me to trim it out for the next flight. To my surprise I only lost the round by one point to a guy who had flown his model for 4-5 years and so knew it inside out. The second round had the same format as the first and I was able to continue trimming the model. As I flew my helper was taking notes as I told him the things I needed to change to make the model more stable. On the third flight the trimming was complete and so I was able to relax, fly the model and enjoy it for the first time. To my utter amazement I won all the rounds bar one but as one round was discarded I achieved a 100% score and won the competition. However, I vowed never to go unprepared again.

In 2007 I returned with the Scout but this time it had more scale detail and was fully trimmed out. Again the model won. In 2008 I added rocket pods and won for the third year running. Following this I had planned to build a new model for the 2009 championship. That model was a BO-105 based on the helicopter owned by Red Bull in Florida, which is used to perform aerobatics at air shows. Unfortunately, one month before the competition, the BO-105 caught fire and I had to bring the Scout out of retirement. Again it won – by a big margin.

The Scout was a special model that I really enjoyed flying. Everything about it was right – whether it was in the air or on the ground. I say was – unfortunately it was destroyed a few weeks after the 2009 US championships at a local fly-in, when the rear tail rotor gearbox failed and it crashed. That's modelling.

Westland Scout military helicopter - four times winner at the US National Championships

Above: Len's Kiowa taking the heat at Heli Heatwave, Texas, USA

A civilian version of the Westland Scout . Could you tell whether this is a model or the real thing?

8. TV and Film Work

I've always liked TV and films and it still amazes me that through this great hobby I was able to see what it was like to be on the other side of the camera.

TV Game Shows

My first appearance came courtesy of Max Coote of Ripmax. One day Max phoned me to ask if I was available. I was, so he asked me to meet him at Elstree aerodrome where we were going to fly to Southampton in his private aeroplane. I duly turned up and put my helicopters into the plane and off we went. On arriving at Southampton, we were met by a car and taken to a TV studio. I was about to make my first TV appearance on the 1980's kids quiz show – Mike Reids Run Around. The format of the show involved the host – Mike Reid - reading out a general knowledge question, to which there were three answers offered on panels at the back of the studio. He would then say "G-g-g-g-go!!", which meant that the kids could run from their little semi-circular home base across to one of panels at the back. Those choosing the right answer would go through to the next round, and so on until there was a winner

For my appearance I was asked to take off in the car park outside of the studio, go inverted and then fly through a number of corridors and into the studio full of children where I was then to flip back the right way up and land. I was horrified when they said children would be present and I pointed out that this would be dangerous as anything could go wrong when flipping back from inverted. I also refused to do any 'normal' flying with the children being around. If they wanted me to fly then the only people who would be around would be me, a helper to guide me and a camera man. They could see I was determined so they agreed and I did the stunt as planned but without anybody else being around.

Imagine my surprise then, when the TV program was transmitted with the children superimposed onto the film to show them sitting around me during the flight sequence. These were obviously put on after I had flown but that was not the way it seemed to those watching the program. Immediately after the show and for some weeks afterwards I had a constant stream of phone-calls from irate people telling me how irresponsible I was. It even included calls from the two leading modelling associations in the UK who were going to take action against me for endangering the kids lives. It took a lot of convincing to prove that the charges were completely false.

ABC Pop Video

When I started this hobby I never would have thought that I - well one of my models - would appear on 'Top of the Pops'. ABC were one of the top pop bands in the UK during the 1980s and I was asked if I could fly a couple of my models on their video for their song 'That was then, but this is now'.

The video featured a map of the world with various national flags on it. This being the height of the cold war between the USA and Russia, the video was to cover a mock battle between two helicopters – one from either side but both supplied and flown by me.

One helicopter was a 'pod and boom' model painted red but as it would only be seen from the front it didn't matter – this was the Russian helicopter. The other model was a scale model representing the USA that would fire rockets (six of them – three from each side of the fuselage) at the Russian intruder.

The rockets were standard household fireworks but without their stabilising sticks or nose cones as they had to fit completely within the rocket tubes on the helicopter. They were fired by electronic detonators. Unfortunately, during the filming of the sequence, one of the rockets hit the stage which then caught fire.

For the final sequence, it had to look as though the US helicopter had shot down the Russian helicopter. To make this more dramatic the Russian helicopter would fly through an 2cm thick, 2 metre square polystyrene sheet that had a timber frame all around it. The filming would take place in front of the polystyrene so that as it broke, pieces would fly in all directions. I was asked to hit the sheet while performing a half roll, so that the model would be on its side when it came through.

There was only one chance to get this right, however, I managed to hit the wooden frame around the edge of the sheet with a rotor blade tip. The sheet broke and I was momentarily blinded by the lights as they shone through the now gaping hole, all of which made landing a bit tricky. Fortunately my automatic reactions kicked in and I managed to land the model on its undercarriage to a standing ovation from the film crew.

It was a good shoot. I still have the US and UK flags from the floor map. You can see the resulting video on You Tube.

James Bond

Having had some exposure on TV, it wasn't long before I was invited to fly on film sets. The very first film was in George Orwell's classic '1984', where I had to fly a Bell 47G in parallel with fellow pilot John Griffiths, who had invited me along.

But of all the film engagements I've done, the most famous were on the set of the James Bond movies. I did three of these which were 'GoldenEye', 'The World is Not Enough' and 'Live and Let Die'.

My involvement started when Nigel Brackley, a good friend of mine who worked at Leavesden film studios, asked me to help them out. At that time Nigel was working on the James Bond film GoldenEye and he asked me if I would make some rotor blades for a quarter scale model they were building for use in the film. The blades would be nearly 2 metres long, 18mm thick and 12cm wide – they wanted six sets of three blades. I produced these on time and must have done a good job as Nigel phoned me up to ask if I would be interested in making moulds for a 2.5 metre long Aerospatiale Squirrel.

I was quite excited at the thought of making these but I didn't want to make the plug that would be used to make the mould. Nigel agreed that they would make the plug - all I had to do was make the mould and build the helicopters from that. There was also a 1.8 metre long model of a new BMW car to be made which I agreed to do as well. Films don't come around that often – particularly prestigious ones such as those involving James Bond!

After a few weeks I went to Leavesden to pick up the plug, but it wasn't until I got back to my workshop that the size of the model made its impact. My workshop is around 3 metre long by 3 metre wide – a 2.5 metre long fuselage takes up an awful lot of that room and I had six of them to make.

As I completed each fuselage I would transport it back to the studios where the house modellers put in the mechanics to make them flyable.

Producing the car was quite interesting. The car company would supply a mould, but as the model was not yet announced, I was given their show model, which was still quite a secret. This model was 100% perfect but in order to take a mould from it, I had to cover it in fibreglass to create the female mould. From this I could then make replicas of the original. As the show model was a one-off, I was very anxious not to damage it. Normally when I take a mould in this way, I coat the model in six layers of polish to protect it from the fibreglass. With this model though I put on ten layers just to be sure.

After the polish I put on the fibreglass and resin mix and waited a couple of hours for it to dry. When I came to pull the now rigid fibreglass mould off the model, I was really scared, but fortunately it came off with no trouble. From this mould I produced six car models. That was it – I'd been paid and that was the end of the job – or so I thought.

A few days later Nigel phoned and asked me if I was busy. I wasn't so he asked me if I would like to fly the models I'd just made. I said I would love to. This was on a Friday morning and I told Nigel that I could sort out my current workload and be with them on Monday. "No" he said, "We want you here within a couple of hours."

I thought he was kidding but he wasn't, so I jumped into my car and went to Leavesdon studio which was around two hours away. Just as I was approaching the studio Nigel called me on my mobile phone to ask me where I was. I told him that I was just entering the main gates to the studio, so he asked me to come straight to the film set.

I got out of the car and said that I could really do with a cup of tea, but Nigel said that there was no time for that as the film producer wanted me right away. The helicopter I was to fly was ready to go with its engine running. I was given the model's transmitter, which fortunately was the same as I used with the switches in the same places. That wasn't so bad but the real issue was that I had never flown the model before, and the flying was to take place outside amongst film equipment, props and dense scenery.

To make matters worse, the helicopter was perched on scaffolding about 2 metres off the ground, on a 1.7 metre square platform that had a slot cut out of it down the middle. Attached to the helicopter – and hanging down the slot, was a 1.7 metre chainsaw with five blades so that as the helicopter took off, the chainsaw would come up through the slot being carried by the helicopter. Because of the height of the platform I couldn't see the top and so I would be blind when judging whether or not the chainsaw had cleared the platform. Other than these minor points it was quite straight-forward. I thought to myself - this is going to be awkward.

There would be two of us flying helicopters for this scene. The person flying the other helicopter says to me "I'll take the right-hand side and you can take the left hand side." For all it was worth this was a bit of relief for me as it meant I could fly a left-hand circuit which, due to the rotation of the blades, is much easier than flying a right hand circuit. My helper told me that the right hand side was much harder to fly as the set had oil rigs and various wires that would need to be avoided for anyone flying in that direction.

Following the cry of "Action!" from the producer, the other pilot took off first, which was then my cue to take off. The helicopter I was flying took off like a dream with no problems at all. But as I was flying towards the left hand side of the set, the other pilot asked me what I was doing. I said that I was positioning myself to be on the left as we had discussed, but he had now changed his mind and he wanted me to fly to the right. This meant I now had to do right-hand circuits with a 2.5 metre model I had never flown before, and I had to avoid all the objects and wires that were on that side.

The director was in radio contact with my helper so that he could pass instructions to us on where he would like us to fly. I was getting the instructions "Get lower", so I drop 1 metre, " Lower", I drop another 2 metres, "Lower still", until finally he said "That's good - hold it there."

I then noticed that the chainsaw I was lifting start to swing – I had hit one of the cables attached between a rig and the ground, but fortunately the wire had came out of the ground so I could carry on.

We did a couple of takes and the model I had was fantastic to fly, even with a chainsaw attached to it. We were then given the all clear to land. As I was the closest to the designated landing spot I came in first. We still had the chainsaws' attached and so to help land there were two sets of scaffolding poles arranged as large wigwam and between these sets of poles was a net onto which the chain saw could be lowered. Once over the net a technician would call out "release" which would indicate we were in the right position and could then hit a switch which would drop the chainsaw from the helicopter into the net. The helicopter could then be landed in the normal way. I went through the procedure with no problems and landed normally.

However, when the technician called "release" to the other flier, rather than hit the switch that would release the cable, the pilot hit the 'engine kill' switch instead. The helicopter sank immediately with the chain saw and 'made love' to one of the scaffolding poles. The resulting crash was spectacular as the model, worth around £20,000, was totally destroyed.

I had done my job and so was no longer needed as the other pilot was scheduled to fly on the other days. As I was about to leave I asked if I could stay for lunch and watch the filming that afternoon. That wasn't a problem and so I stayed on. The other pilot was due to see the director that afternoon to discuss a number of other stunts he was due to fly, including picking up a portacabin with the helicopter . I thought – lucky bugger, I'd love to do that.

After lunch the director asked who was going to do the flying. The other pilot spoke up to which the director asked "Are you the idiot who crashed the helicopter this morning?". When he confirmed that he was, the director said "You're not flying - he is" and pointed to me. "Be here early in the morning"

I was speechless – as was the other pilot. Before going home I was given instructions of what they wanted. On the producers pad it said 'one helicopter, one pilot' and in brackets 'Len Mount'. Evidently this was very unusual as, I was told later, they don't name the pilots. So the other pilot was now my helper – he was there to support me. I did have some fun with him by making it difficult for him to start the model. I ended up with 10 days work - the only time I have ever got work through someone else crashing.

Shaken but not stirred

On one scene for the film 'The World is Not Enough', I had to fly a large model over the top of a camera that was mounted on a 6 metre high platform. The director told me that I was to skim over the cameraman's head as if I was going downhill. As it would be rather dangerous to fly from the ground, I asked the director if it would be possible for me to be up there on the same level as the camera. This would be much safer as I would be able to better judge that height and could therefore fly much closer to the camera.

He agreed to this so I told my helper to grab my belt. The plan was that as I took off from the ground, he could then walk me backwards up the steps on the platform. There were three tiers of steps and I would have to negotiate corners while flying, which was quite awkward. I couldn't take off from the top of the stairs, as I wouldn't be able to see the attitude of the helicopter, so walking up the stairs so I could be the same height as the helicopter was the only way I could do it.

This worked well but when doing low passes and it was absolutely frightening. I was near the cameraman so I had to fly the model right at me. As the model came closer and closer, it was getting bigger and bigger. You don't realise how big it is until it's right on top of you. As it passes over head, close to the camera is was only a metre or so away. I consider myself to be a good flyer but even for me this was a bit close.

As soon as the helicopter was past the camera, all I had to do was to take off pitch to bring it down, which gave the effect that it was flying down hill. After a couple of passes I said to my helper that I had got a problem – the tail has gone. He didn't believe me as the model wasn't pirouetting. I told him again, "the tail has gone – its not working". I had already hit the low gyro switch, which was making no difference at all – I had no tail control and so I couldn't turn it around.

As that particular film shot was complete, I decided to grab some height before attempting to bring the model back to me. I was already downwind so I warned my helper that it would start pirouette as soon as I came into wind. And sure enough, as soon as I came into wind it started to pirouette. But fortunately, unlike a normal radio control helicopter where the pirouettes would be fast, this one was nice and slow.

I couldn't stop it turning so I grabbed some more height by opening up the throttle, while at the same time I looked around to see where I could land. I saw some space about 800 metres away so I informed my helper that I would cut the engine and do an autorotation landing. What I had forgotten was that after the previous crash, we had disconnected the engine kill switch to prevent that happening again, so the engine couldn't be turned off. As I started the autorotation manoeuvre I hit the engine kill switch and the machine came in to land – but unbeknown to me was that the engine was still running.

I misjudged the landing spot and it came down behind a hedge, out of my view. I thought I would flare out the landing by adding in more pitch, even though it was now out of view. To my surprise the helicopter that had disappeared, now reappeared again this time climbing into the air from behind the hedge. Right away I realised that the engine was still running. So I put in full left and decided to roll it into the ground – things were too dangerous to let it fly away.

We heard the helicopter hit the ground so we went from our flying position, through a gap in the fence to find the 'crashed' helicopter. On other side of the hedge wasn't a field but a road, that had another hedge on its far side. When we got there we found a young guy leaning against his pick-up truck. "Wow man", he said, "that was a drive and a half!" I asked him what he meant and he said, "Well I was doing 90kph down this road when all of a sudden I saw this helicopter right in front of me, looking at me. I stopped my truck but as I got out, it took off again and flew into the hedge."

I was only too relieved that it hadn't hit him. I'm sure it's one of those things he'll never forget.

We picked up the helicopter and found to our surprise, that the only damage was a broken blade and a bent a fly bar – the rest was perfectly ok. On further investigation we found that the guy who built the model (he was also the person who had crashed previously) had installed a 3-stage belt drive to the tail. The gearbox was held by an aluminium bracket with 3mm bolts and underneath this was a bracket secured by blind nuts. However, he had forgotten to put in the blind nuts and as a result the gearbox moved just enough causing the tail belts to slip occasionally – and that's why we were getting slow pirouettes.

Blown Up

One scene that was particularly impressive was at night where the helicopters were going to get blown up. I practiced during the day with a pod and boom helicopter to get the angles and distance right. During this time we had someone take the directors place as he was on the camera checking out the film shots. The practice involved flying the helicopter over water, stopping in line with the director, turning and then flying forwards towards him.

We got it pretty good – but the real director had never practiced it. What they didn't tell me was that the model was going to be full up of explosives – if I had known I wouldn't have stood so close on take off. As well as the explosives the model was to take off with a chainsaw attached.

Actual filming started around midnight. I took off from a trailer – the model was on one end and I was at the other end in a 1.3 metre square hide. This was made out of 4x4 timber and 3cm thick Perspex to protect me should anything go wrong. It was also there to protect me from the explosives, although I didn't know this at that time.

During the day flying wasn't a problem as I could see thought the windows, however at night the window I was looking through lit up from the glare of the lights and I had trouble seeing through it. I told my helper to hang onto me as I was going to lean outside of the hide, and to pull me in as soon as he heard the explosion, so I didn't get any shrapnel.

I took off and flew along waiting to be given the signal by the director to stop, turn 90 degrees and then fly forward. I flew along, the director called "stop", but as anyone who flies helicopters knows, you can't just stop as it takes a bit of time to slow down.

"You've missed the mark", yelled the director and so we had to do it again. This took a couple of takes before we got it right.

Now the director has the button to trigger the explosives, as he is the one who decides exactly when things are to blow up. To make the explosion even more dramatic I was to fly between a V structure where propane gas was being pumped out. The idea being to explode the helicopter in this V structure to dramatically increase the explosion effect.

It was up to the director to press it at the right time, however, on the take he pressed the button far too early and the effect was lost. The director goes ballistic and after looking at the rushes, shouts at me "You bloody fool - you weren't far enough forward." "I'm sorry", I said, "I was travelling forward but you are the one with the button – you didn't have to press it that early."

One of the director's assistants pulled me to one side and told me that I couldn't speak to the director like that. I replied that I wasn't going to take the blame for what was clearly his mistake. Filming stopped while we had a sandwich and a cup of tea, after which the director came up to me and apologised. He said that he was sorry, that it was his fault and that he had accused me in the heat of the moment. "No problems", I said and so we went to film the scene again.

We got out a new £20,000 model and I took off. This time things went perfectly and the director was right on cue. The explosion that followed was superb, it couldn't have been any better. The noise was unbelievable. At the time I had my head out of the door of the hide as I couldn't see properly through the safely glass. My helper should have pulled me back but didn't because the intensity of the explosion and the rocking that followed took him by surprise. Just as I pulled my head in you could feel and hear the bits of the model hitting the Perspex window, so I guess I was pretty damn lucky.

The next morning they fished the blown up model out of the water and found it was completely destroyed. It's interesting that I'm sad when my own models get destroyed but not this time. I had been paid to build the model, so it was theirs and not mine.

When I saw the finished film at the premier in London, it was fantastic to see what they had done with the model flying sequences. They had superimposed people sitting in the helicopter firing machine guns, none of which were in the original model. It looked so real.

9: Retirement

I guess none of us likes to think that we're getting near to the end of our careers, particularly when it's something we really like to do. But as we get older, things overtake us and we are soon left with little choice. I always wanted to stop while at the top of my game, rather than become some poor 'old boy' who was simply living off his old achievements.

I had suffered a number of heart attacks in 1996 that had threatened to end my career several years earlier. At that time I had entered the team trials for the European aerobatic championships, which were planned to take place in the middle of winter. In some respects it should never have been held as it was far too cold and there was risk of the tail blades icing up and coming off.

To qualify for the team, you don't have to win it to qualify – just come in the first three places, with 4th place being for a reserve pilot.

I went to the trials with a helper from my local model club. The first round I won easily and was quite confident I could win overall. While waiting for the next round I said to my helper that we should grab a coffee and a bacon sandwich to warm up. We had just started on our food when the organiser came up to us and told us we were on next. I disagreed and told him that I wasn't due to fly unless he had changed the flying order. He said that he hadn't and that if I didn't like it I could go home.

So I gobbled down my sandwich and coffee and went to the ready box. Right away I didn't feel well and had chest pains. I thought I had indigestion caused by eating my sandwich too fast. I started the helicopter and flew it to the competition pad but I had no idea where I was or what I was doing. I was so out of it I even asked my helper what switches to operate. The round didn't go well and I came last. My chest was starting to hurt so much that it was hard to bear.

I would be last in the next round, so decided to go and warm up as it would be an hour or so before I was needed next. I went to the car and switched on the heater and slept. I went out for the third round and won it, and as only two rounds count for qualification, I had won the team trials.

A few months later I had similar chest pains and I was continually out of breath, so I went to see my doctor who arranged a hospital appointment the following week. When I arrived there they hooked me up to an ECG machine that revealed that I had had a heart attack, and quite a big one. It also showed that this wasn't the first. The doctor immediately phoned Guys hospital in London to arrange an angiogram and said to the person setting the appointments "… forget two weeks time – he's leaving right now".

Evidently I was having another heart attack while lying on the bed. When I arrived at Guys they found that I had three blockages for which they inserted three stents right away. This was on a Thursday. I was quite concerned as I was due to be at the Sandown Park show on the Saturday, which for me was my main sales event for the year. So Olive and a couple of the lads from my flying club came to the hospital on the Friday morning and told me not to worry as they would set up the stand for me on the Friday night.

I was discharged from hospital later that day and got a taxi home, which cost me a fortune. I arrived to an empty house as everyone else was at Sandown Park setting up for the show. When they arrived home later that night they told me that everything was alright for the following day and I should stay at home and take it easy. This wasn't in my nature so once they saw I was determined to attend, my daughter hired a wheelchair and I went.

Selling the business

Although I made a swift recovery, I knew that I would need to stop at some stage. But I kept putting things off. A few years later I was diagnosed with diabetes and although I kept pretty active, I was finding it hard to keep up the punishing schedule of being both a manufacturer and a competition pilot

In 2006 - I had just turned 64 - I decided that I would officially retire at 65. I had built up a stock of fuselage moulds for a range of models and it didn't seem right to confine them to a skip as I had done with the rotor blades. I was also still receiving a stream of enquiries for scale fuselages and so it seemed only right to sell the business as a going concern. But it had to be to the right person – someone who understood how to treat the moulds and to make the perfect body.

I had spent hundreds of hours making each mould as near perfect as I could and it was important to me that customers would benefit from that skill. It's very easy to destroy a mould and produce inferior results, and as my name was on the final product I wanted to preserve not only my reputation but also give customers value for money.

I put my scale helicopter manufacturing business on the market, which was eventually bought by a friend of mine in the US – Al Wert of Starwood Models. He took the moulds that I had used, together with spare fuselages, mechanics and various other components. I spent a few weeks with him at his home showing him how I build the models – and then that was it. I was now officially retired.

So what was I going to do? I had spent the last 35 years building model helicopters and so it seemed only reasonable that in my retirement I would build …. more model helicopters! Only this time I would tackle subjects that were different and that intrigued me. These wouldn't be to make a living but would be 'one-off' models chosen simply because I wanted to build them. Within a few days of retirement I had a number projects on the go – here are three of them.

Notar

The first project was the Hiller J10 – or more commonly known as the Notar (short for No Tail Rotor). The project came about when Al Wert invited me to go to a full size air show called 'Circumgiration' – a fly-in held in San Francisco each year.

Al had put on a display of model helicopters, both static and flying, which proved to be popular with the crowd. While there he took me to the Hiller museum that traces the history of the famous helicopter designer. As we looked around I noticed, hanging from the ceiling, a helicopter that looked like a big long cigar or pear drop. I found out that it was built in 1947, with the prototype dating from 1945. This was in the real early days of helicopter flight. It was so impressive that I took a number of photos of it.

Once I got back home and looked through the photos it dawned on me that it would make a great challenge to build a scale model of it. I phoned Al and asked him if there was any chance of getting close up photos of the helicopter – as I could only get them from the ground. So he went back to the museum and after speaking to them they put up some scaffolding so he could take some close up photos as well as take detailed measurements.

As the model didn't make production – in fact the machine never flew – there were no 3-view drawings available. So when I received the photos from Al, I scaled them up to make my own diagram. I did this by placing a spare set of mechanics that I had, along with a turbine engine onto a length of wallpaper and drew round them while attempting to keep the outline of the fuselage. Although the original was petrol driven, I chose a turbine engine as I wanted to use the thrust of the engine to keep the tail in place, rather than use a fan as most people do with this kind of model. Once I had the right proportions I took one of the photos of the full-size helicopter to a printer and asked him to scale it up to the size I had on the wallpaper. The result became the basis of the plans for the model.

Now the project was gathering momentum, I phoned Al to see whether the museum would be interested in the model once it was complete. They were and what's more they agreed to pay for me to attend the following years' event with the finished model.

To begin with the build was a slow process as I had plenty of time. I was due to have it finished for June 2007 but as is normal in life, other things got in the way and I missed the date. I visited Al in January 2008 and went to the museum, who said they were having another show in June 2008 and that they would be looking forward to seeing the model then. With only five months to go, the project was now urgent.

One of the main problems I had yet to tackle was to work out how to use the thrust from the turbine to control the tail. The exhaust from a jet engine is in the region of 600C and anything in the way – such as a servo or control wires – were going to melt, or at the very least expand and destroy any delicate movement that I needed. I didn't even know if there would be sufficient thrust from the engine. To solve these problems I created a test bed consisting of a flat plank and a tail tube through which the exhaust gases flowed. I named it the 'ironing board'.

It was made to be the same width and length as the finished model. The exhaust 'tube' was 1.3 metre long that finished in a set of 'vanes' that could direct the exhaust either left or right. This was initially controlled by a servo but to help with the C of G I mounted the servo in the centre of the board and ran tracing wire down tail to operate an actuating arm by the vanes. These were about 1.4 metre long and I thought the intense heat of the exhaust would not affect them.

On the first flight the model started to pirouette and I was not able to bring it under control. I thought the angle of the tail vents was wrong and found that the heat from the exhaust tube had expanded the wires operating the vanes so that they had become very slack and of no use. To overcome this I decided to fit carbon push-pull rods to operate the tail as they wouldn't go slack but unfortunately the heat melted them.

Another solution was to put the servo at the back of the tail and used 12cm push rods to operate the control, surface. This worked perfectly but as the model flew I noticed the exhaust tube was starting to buckle. On investigation I found that because I had anchored the exhaust tube at the front as well as the back of the 'plank', the tremendous heat had made it expand but the only way it could move was sideways, hence it buckled over 4cm in the middle. To overcome this I had to make the exhaust tube a sliding fit – the back would be anchored but would fit over another exhaust tube, which was anchored at the front. This meant it could expand but without any buckling. This final fix worked well.

Another problem is that the fuselage is so big it required two people to man handle the plug from which the mould is then taken. I've never had anything that large or heavy before. I had to put it on a trolley to move it around the shed as I couldn't pick it up.

I managed to finish the model with two weeks to go - just enough time to test fly it. It flew OK although it was strange not seeing any tail rotor. It was then boxed up and taken to the US where it made its debut. It did generate some interest mainly because it was so unusual. It even appeared on the local TV news channel who showed it flying.

I was expecting the museum to buy it at the end of the show, but due to a change in personnel they didn't seem interested. So to save taking it back to the UK, Al bought it from me. To my knowledge it is the only flying model of this interesting subject.

Lego 'Sea Rescue' Helicopter

The models I build have to be different and unique. I want them to have a 'wow' factor either because they are rare or because of the detail I will put in. But it is getting more and more difficult finding these unique subjects. Then one day a good friend of mine, Michael Coveney,

Above: The 'ironing board' used to detemine directional thrust control
Below: The J10 prototype in the air

Above: A young boy chooses between the real thing and the one that flies
Below: Len Mount Tomahawk - jet powered aerobatic 'pod and boom' model

asked me if I could help him out with an unusual project. He had been dabbling in radio control helicopters for 20 years or more but like me, wanted to have something different. Back in the early days he had wanted to build a 'scale' model of a Lego brick 'sea rescue' helicopter but it hadn't got any further than an idea.

As I was in regular contact with him, he asked me how to approach such a project. He had bought an original 1986 Lego brick model from eBay, and had enlarged top and side-view photographs of the model so that the mechanics of an Align T-Rex 500 would fit inside. Right away, the thought of building and flying a scale Lego helicopter caught my imagination. Rather than just advise Michael, I found myself being drawn in to creating a wooden mockup and turning it into a mould. Within two weeks I had built the helicopter and fitted it out with mechanics, radio and a 4 blade 'scale' rotor head.

The first few flights were 'interesting' and it became obvious that it needed an electronic stabilizer. With this fitted, it flew fine. The reaction we get at shows is amazing and is a definite hit. Most children (and quite a few adults) instantly recognize the model as 'Lego' and they soon gather round it smiling and talking about it. I'm tempted to enter it in at a scale competition – the rules don't say you can't scale up a model, and it is accurate even down to the pilot and 'nobbles' on the bricks! It definitely has the 'wow' factor – you can see it flying on YouTube. All it needs now is a companion – maybe I should build the other helicopters in the Lego range?

Red Bull BO105

After winning at the 2008 US Nationals for the third time, I wanted to go back 'one last time' to defend my title, but with a model that would 'wow' both spectators and fellow competitors. It had to be 'special' not only in looks but also in the way it performed. Although the nationals had only been over for a day, I discussed with friends at the hotel as to what I could do, when the subject of 'the Red Bull helicopter' came up. For those who are not familiar with this helicopter, Red Bull own a couple of BO-105's that are certified for aerobatics. They fly these at various events around the world and are the highlight of any show. Check out some of the videos on YouTube.

I thought it would be great to build a model that could not only win a scale competition but also would not disgrace itself in an aerobatic competition. With this in mind I set out to research the model.

Although it's easy to find information and diagrams on the BO105, I really had to see the real thing and take close-up photos of it. Once back in the UK I contacted Red Bull as I knew the helicopter would be appearing at the London Red Bull air races. Despite a few phone calls it became apparent that returning calls from a 'crank' like myself was very much a low priority.

I managed to work out the size of the model by placing a set of mechanics on a sheet of wall paper and then drawing round the profile of the 105, but unless I could measure and photograph the full size version the project would soon come unstuck.

A friend of mine suggested we write a letter to Dieter Mateschitz the owner of Red Bull who lives in Austria. We put together an overview of what we were trying to do along with photos from previous projects. To my amazement I received a reply from Harald Reiter who manages the Red Bull 'Flying Bulls', which includes their aerobatic helicopters. My letter to Dieter had been passed onto Harald who took an interest in the project.

Harald said that he would allow me access to the helicopters - they have two in the US and two based in Austria. My friend Al of Starwood Models lives fairly close to the one based in California so without any delay I booked my flight.

On arriving at the airfield where the BO105 is kept, I was met by Charles 'Chuck' Aaron, who is the only FAA-certified helicopter stunt pilot and a master at making a helicopter do things 'it isn't supposed to do'. He taught himself how to fly the aerobatic routine he performs at air shows in the Red Bull helicopter and is a typical comic book hero with his extravagant moustache and blonde hair. Within a few minutes he asked me if I would like to go with him on a test flight following routine maintenance on the 105. I didn't need to be asked twice. Having been strapped in the seat of a very sparse cockpit, Chuck took off and informed me that none of the maneuvers he was about to do would be violent. "Violent?" I thought, " What could be violent in a simple maintenance flight?"

It wasn't long before I found out as Chuck then performed a series of aerobatic maneuvers that forced my head from one side of the cockpit to the other. A roll to the left, a stall-turn followed by a loop. Initially it was quite unnerving and I closed my eyes during the first roll but then I thought to myself "what are you doing - this is an opportunity of a lifetime". I made sure that I kept them open for the rest of the flight, which included Chuck's full aerobatic schedule.

After what seemed like just a few minutes, an alarm went off in the cockpit. "Oh don't worry about that", said Chuck calmly, " It's just the fuel warning sensor telling us we're running out". With that Chuck headed for the airfield a couple of miles away. On the way back he asked me what maneuver I liked the least. Without hesitation I said "roll" at which point Chuck put the helicopter into a tight left-hand roll. Over went my head to one side and the earth outside the cockpit rotated.

After landing, I got out of the cockpit with one of the biggest smiles I've ever had. Chuck came over to me, shook my hand and thanked me. I asked him why he was thanking me to which he replied that it was for not throwing up as it saved him from having to clean the interior. It was the best flight I have ever experienced.

I spent the next couple of hours taking around 800 photos but when I got back to the UK, I found that I still needed more for areas I had missed. I got back in contact with Harald in

Side view of Len's stunning PJW jet powered, fully aerobatic, Red Bull BO-105.
Now in the Red Bull museum in Salzburg, Austria

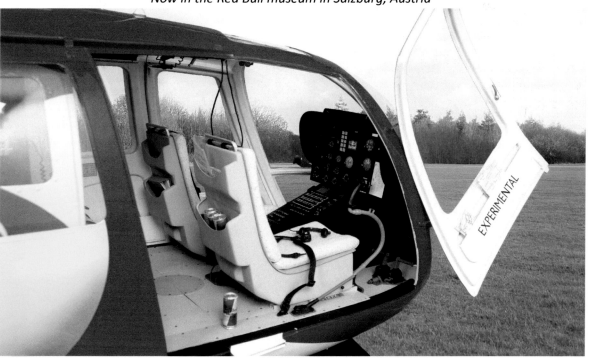

Inside the BO-105 is just as good as the outside. Even the drink cans are to scale.

91

Len walks after the BO-105 with its purpose built radio-controlled tractor unit, complete with flashing lights and a driver that nods and waves to the crowd.

Austria who invited me over to look around their version in Salzburg. I went with a friend and we were treated like VIP guests.

The Flying Bulls have two magnificent glass hangers at Salzburg airport. One is open to the public and contains a selection of historic aircraft and some of the F1 Red Bull racing cars. Aircraft include a Douglas DC-6, B-25J Mitchell bomber, Cessna Amphibian Caravan, Corsair, Bell 47, Cobra and a squadron of Alpha Jets. And a BO105 CB.

The other aircraft hanger is where they maintain the aircraft and store others. It is an amazing place and well worth the visit. Having taken the photos I returned to the UK to build the model. You can read in detail how I did this in the second half of this book, which is dedicated to building a high quality scale model helicopter.

Although I finished the model, it wasn't all straightforward. On its maiden test flight I had just started up the turbine engine when something backfired and set light to the propane gas cylinder in the fuselage. Within seconds the model was engulfed in flames and I immediately shut everything down. The damage was extensive. It destroyed most of the cabling and electronics, as well as making a complete mess of the paintwork and mechanics. Repairs took a further year to effect - only this time I installed an on-board fire extinguisher.

The resulting model is impressive – and big. In fact it is so big it really doesn't fit in my house and is a nightmare to transport on my own. The solution was to build another one, only this time a bit smaller. So that's what I did – I now have two BO-105 machines.

Return to Europe

As retirement gradually dawns on me, I've started to get back to visiting the more informal fly-in I used to attend at the start of my career. It is here you meet the genuine enthusiast – those that are not driven by commercial interests or who are wanting to build a name for themselves. These shows also tend to be smaller so there is time to meet, exchange stories and make new friends.

Two of the events that come to mind occurred in Holland and Germany.

Joop Van Lent is a fellow competitor from the first F3C European Championships held in Eibergen, Holland in 1984. Joop emailed me in Spring 2010 'out of the blue' and asked me if I would like to go to Eibergen for a fun fly he was organizing. I hadn't spoke to Joop for over 15 years, but we had got on well with each other. It sounded like a good idea and as I had had enough of the pressure of competitions, getting back to see some of my old friends was very appealing.

I loaded up my car with models, camping gear and a friend and made the trip to Holland. From where I live it only took five hours so I arrived still fresh. It was great to see Joop again and we were soon engaged in story telling as though we had met every week without a gap.

We spent two days there, camping at night, flying during the day and just having a great time.

While there I got talking to someone I hadn't met before - Kay Matthiesem from Germany who was flying a turbine powered BO-105. The conversation soon turned to my own experiences in building the Red Bull BO105, and Kay expressed an interest in buying a fuselage from me. He also invited me to a fly-in he was arranging in Niederrheim, Germany a few months later.

Having had such a great time in Holland, I went to Kay's show and was equally impressed. Everyone I met was so friendly and enthusiastic. Unlike shows in the UK, these events are for all the family and so those flying brought along their wives and kids as well. There was plenty for them to do and the clubhouses offered, warmth, great food and a chance for them to enjoy themselves outside of the subject of radio control helicopters.

At Kay's show in particular, the standard of models and flying was excellent. I even met a person who had one of my original Huey helicopter kits and had done a fantastic job on it. The cockpit instruments had been fitted with over 100 minute bulbs telling me that I had met someone who was more obsessed than me. I had such a great time that I'm planning on going back to these and other events next year.

Retirement?

As I said at the start of this chapter, none of us likes to think we are at the end of our careers. And I guess I've come to accept that although I'm officially 'retired', I'm still just as busy and committed to building scale helicopters as I've always been.

I have a sign in my building room that says "God put me on this earth to finish a certain number of projects. Right now I am so far behind I will never die".

At this very moment I'm working on two projects – a smaller BO-105 that I can actually carry and a Cobra military helicopter that will be painted in Red Bull colours. Oh – and I also have some plans to build another Lego model. After these, there are bound to be more. I guess I'm not ready to stop or die anytime soon.

PART TWO

Building a Championship Winning Scale Model

In this second part of this book, I would like to show you how I build a scale model that's capable of winning competitions at an international level. The following chapters cover the approach I take and some of the techniques I use to produce models that, apart from size, are indistinguishable from the real thing.

None of these techniques are difficult to master or expensive to carry out. Most of my models are made out of scrap materials and have been constructed in the confines of a 3 metre x 3 metre bedroom, which has become my workshop.

To provide continuity, these chapters follow the building of the Red Bull BO105 helicopter that resides in California. However, some pictures included in the text are from other models, as these show off the techniques better than those I did for the BO105.

Books of this nature are limited in space when it comes to showing photographs and so an accompanying CD is provided which contains far more illustrations than can be accommodated within these pages.

Just one final word – I am obsessed by scale detail as you will see in the following pages. But you don't have to be to build an impressive model. As you go through these chapters, don't be put off by my excesses. I've had 40+ years to develop them, so feel free to skip or ignore areas that you think are way over the top to accomplish. After all this is a hobby, and hobbies should be fun.

Enjoy your building.

Len Mount

10. Getting Started

Tackling scale models

In building a new scale model I like to find a helicopter that no one – or very few - has done before. If you think about a Jet Ranger, nearly every model manufacturer has one in their range. But very few, for example have done a large Huey, and no one had done the N4 Dauphin before I attempted to build either of these. As a result the models I produced were unique and were bound to grab the attention of a judge in a scale competition.

But perhaps the most important criteria for choosing a machine to model, has to be your love for the subject. I am a fast builder and I am able to devote most of my time to producing a model, but even then it will take me anything from 6 months to 2 years to take a model from a basic drawing to a flying machine that can win.

For me a scale model is exactly that. It has to be scale in every detail right down to the nuts and bolts and that means accuracy. I hate it when I see so called scale models that have doors and exhaust grills in the wrong place; where lettering doesn't use the right font, or the paint is a different colour.

And I get particularly critical when I can see the radio and engine inside the fuselage where there should be seats, controls and an instrument panel. It is quite common for me to spend as much time in getting the inside detail right as it is on the outside. This even extends to the way in which the door handles work, the inside door pocket compartments and various detailing hidden behind closed hatches.

On some of my models I have been accused of cheating when judges have seen the photos I've submitted of the full size aircraft, and claimed that I must have taken a photo of the model and substituted it for the full size photo. At the last US National competition where I entered my military Westland Scout, after 15 minutes of studying the full size photos and my model, they judges were unable to spot one error. It won the competition by a huge margin.

I guess I am obsessed with accuracy and my achievements are probably the result of that obsession. But before I put you off, I have to tell you that my models are rarely perfect at the start. For me, the initial building of a model is just the start. Once I have a completed model I then work on it over the years to perfect it.

The Scout mentioned above had four years of development on it from the initial build. Each year my friends and I would study the model and photos of the full size, noting any discrepancies. I would then adjust the model until they were eradicated. As you can see, to build a model to this high standard, it must be a love affair.

Choosing the Subject

Most of the models I build take a minimum of 500 hours that can span several years during which time I will encounter many challenges. But if the model is something that I really want to build then I don't mind spending the time and the effort to make sure I do a good job.

The Red Bull BO105 aerobatic helicopter is a great example of an interesting subject. I flew FAI F3C aerobatics for many years and won numerous competitions in that discipline, so the thought of flying an aerobatic schedule in a scale class intrigued me. This alone would be enough to raise a few eyebrows, which I always find an incentive. Then there is the machine itself – the BO105 is a nice looking machine and has room for a turbine engine which is typically my power plant of choice. It has a large cabin area with double doors that will give easy access when installing a scale interior. Finally, the Red Bull colour scheme is bright, attractive and instantly recognisable. However that does mean I will need to do a good job on the scale detail as there are more people who will notice any errors or inaccuracies.

Having chosen a suitable subject, you then need to decide on whether you are going to make the fuselage from scratch or buy a commercially available body and adapt it for use. When I first started out in scale modelling I would use a commercial kit and modify the body so that it was true to scale. I would do this by altering things like filling in the windows and cutting out new ones that were the right shape and in the right place. I would also add more scale detail that was on the original but missing in the kit.

The advantage of this approach is that someone else has already worked out where the mechanics, engine and radio will fit and, if you are not used to making moulds, will save a great deal of time and heartache. The downside is that most kits are not that accurate, you may find that the interior space is lacking and you are limited in the size of the finished model. However, there is no reason why a kit model cannot be turned into a world-class championship-winning model.

Having mastered the techniques of building moulds I always build my own. It means I can make the body very accurate and I have total control over the size and amount of scale detail I want to build into the model. For something like the BO-105, building the mould took me around 350 hours – and as I now have the mould I can quickly make replacement parts or even a completely new body in a matter of days should I want to.

If you choose to buy a ready-made body, the internet is a good place to search for suitable kits. There are the large manufacturers who will sell you a standard set of mechanics for which a scale body is available, however these are not always that good. For more accurate body kits there are a few specialist vendors such as Century or Starwood Models in the US, and Heli-Factory in Germany, but these do come at a price.

Model Research

Having chosen a subject, we now need to research the model in more detail. Depending on the kind of competition you want to enter, you will need to make sure you can produce all the documentary evidence the contest directors will require. As I enter many national competitions I have to supply a booklet containing multiple close-up views of both the interior and exterior, as well as scale 3-view drawings.

In addition, you will also need many, many photos of the full-size helicopter to help with putting on the scale detail. For the Red Bull BO105 I took over 1200 photos – and I still found I hadn't got enough for some parts of the bodywork. This means that ideally, the full size version of the subject should be accessible so you can get up close to it.

Again the best place to start your research is the Internet. Fortunately for me, there were many photos of the Red Bull helicopter in action including video footage that was useful for determining the scale flight manoeuvres I would perform. I also looked up the manufacturer and found quite a bit of material on the model types and overall dimensions which were useful in keeping the model in proportion.

It was here that I found out where the full-size was kept and contact details of the owner. There is no substitute to being able to see the real thing close up and taking your own photographs.

Power Plants

At this stage it's worthwhile talking about how the model will be powered. To my mind a scale model has to look right and sound right. Having a beautifully built model that sounds like a chainsaw with blue smoke pouring from the bottom destroys the illusion we are trying to create.

Gas turbine engines sound just like the real thing. They start and the blades spool up just like the real thing with the added bonus is that there is no smoke or mess to clear up afterwards. But they are expensive and potentially lethal in the hands of an inexperienced pilot.

An alternative to turbine power is in the new breed of electric motors. The right combination of motor, speed controller and Li-Poly battery will give you enough power to fly the largest of scale models. The electric whine of the motor is similar to a turbine engine and if you use a clutch so that the motor has to get up to speed before the blades turn, the illusion is complete.

A word of warning though on electric. The new generation of Li-Poly batteries and motors can also be lethal. They require careful handling, particularly when charging and if for some reason you manage to short out the battery, you will have a fire just as destructive as any petrol fire. I know – I've burnt out quite a few models this way. In addition, getting the right combination of motor, gearing, battery and speed controller is essential – get it wrong and you can end up with an expensive BBQ or something that won't fly. There are formulae for working this out but you are far better off finding out what others are using successfully for something that is similar in size and weight to what you are planning, and then copying that.

While an electric setup is not cheap, the purchase cost is still significantly lower than a turbine. When I started the Red Bull helicopter I decided to use a power plant I was familiar with, hence I stayed with a Jakadofsky turbine engine.

Having chosen the power plant we now need to plan how the engine will take in fresh air, how it will stay cool and how the exhaust gases (if any) are to be expelled. For me this means printing out a side view of the proposed model to the size I plan to build, and then laying on the paper the mechanics and power plant to work out where I need to provide air intakes and exhaust ducts.

With a scale model you may not have a choice where the exhaust exits, but if you have to cut holes to allow air in and out, you can at least plan them to be in places (e.g. under the cabin floor) where it doesn't stand out to those viewing the model sitting on its undercarriage. For the smaller Red Bull BO105 I built, this meant routing the exhaust through the back part of the cabin. To hide this from the side I put in dark windows at the back of the cabin, and to hide it from the front of the model, I put in a cabin wall behind the seats. Although this is not scale, it is better to see an uncluttered area without an exhaust system, than one that is obviously not scale. On the larger Red Bull BO105, there was enough room to route the exhaust and keep it out of the cabin area altogether.

Rotor Head and Mechanics

The easiest route when considering the rotor head and mechanics is to buy a commercial set. The head needs to look scale and should not have a fly-bar as this will loose points in a competition. It will also mean purchasing an electronic stabilizing system so that hovering and slow flight manouvers are kept realistic.

I make all my own mechanics, mainly because when I started there were no kits and so you had to make everything yourself. I used to machine my own rotor heads but these days I have a friend with a CNC lathe and milling machine, which makes the job a bit easier.

Today, I have a basic set of side frames, swash-plates and rotor heads, which I then tailor for each machine I build. If you go commercial then choose a set of mechanics that you know works. Although most manufacturers do not make scale heads, (I subsequently found that M-copter does have one for a BO105), you can add extra detail to them to give a more scale like appearance.

For example, you can get rid of the manufacturers marks by sanding them off and modifying the bolts that retain the blades, by machining cups that the bolts will fit into. With the BO105 you can add the blade weights and put sleeves on the push rods that connect the swash-plate to the blade holders so they appear to be more like the real thing.

Just painting the whole rotor head assembly along with the blades will make it look better and earn you more points. On the subject of blades I always make my own but I wouldn't recommend this route as there are many good quality blades around these days at a reasonable cost.

For the tail rotor gearbox I often add body filler and sculpt the unit to shape. On my Westland Scout I used body filler to create a housing for the rear flashing light. For the tail rotor blades buy a set that are as close as possible to the full size in shape and size and then paint them.

11. Making the Body Shell

This chapter is for those people who want to build their own fuselage. It assumes that you have a basic knowledge of fibre-glassing techniques and a little understanding of the materials involved. If you already have a fuselage you can skip this section and move onto Chapter 12 – Completing the Body.

The way I build a body is to first make a 'plug' that will then be used to create a mould. The mould is then used to form the main body and panels. In terms of materials I make the moulds out of fibreglass matting and polyester resin, while the finished parts are made from cloth and epoxy resin.

The reason for this is that epoxy resin is more expensive than polyester, but just as important, parts made from epoxy release more easily from a polyester mould.

Determining Size

Having decided to make your own fuselage, the next step is to decide how big to make it. As part of the decision-making process I like to determine how the mechanics and power plant will fit into the body, which then determines the overall size of the model. For me, a detailed interior is a must therefore I have to make sure that the mechanics and power plant will not intrude into the cabin, or if they do that they don't take too much away from the interior that can be shown.

The best way to do this is to get a roll of wallpaper and place the set of mechanics you intend to use, onto it. I then draw the outline of the chosen subject around the mechanics to see where things will fit. To draw an accurate outline requires printing a side view of the helicopter. A search of the Internet will soon reveal outlines for most helicopters – it doesn't have to be a good resolution as we only want a rough guide to the outline.

I then draw a grid over the outline and transfer this to a larger grid on the wall paper that has the mechanics. From this I now have the overall size of the model from which I can decide whether I have a room big enough to build it, and just as important, that will fit into my motor vehicle for transportation when built.

For the Red Bull BO105, I already had a set of mechanics from my own design Odyssey machine, which I used to work out how big the model would need to be with this setup. In my case this equated to a model that would be 76cm high, 61cm wide and 232cm long. (Although this doesn't sound that big, it's huge when trying to move it around). To ensure that it would fit into my vehicle, as well as making it easier to build, I decided to make the body in two parts – the main body and the tail section. These would be bolted together for flight so I had to make sure that the couplings for tail drive as well as electrical systems would go together simply while being absolutely reliable.

Making the Plug

The first step in making the plug is to turn the side view of the helicopter into one made from MDF. This can be done by cutting out the paper side-view created above, and tracing round it onto a large piece of board. A few minutes with a jig-saw will soon see the job done.

The next step is to turn this 'flat' view into 3D by adding formers to each side of the MDF profile. The technique I use is to divide the side-view drawing into sections – nose, cabin front, cabin rear, main shaft, rear body and tail – for the BO-105 I used seven sections.

To get the profile of each former right, I bought a plastic kit of the full-size model and cut the half side body into the same sections I had drawn on the MDF profile.

I then traced the profile of each section onto paper and measured the height of each piece and compared it to the height of the corresponding section on the MDF board, I now use a photocopier to blow up the traced image until the height is the same size as the height on the corresponding MDF section. If the size I want is too big for the photocopier, I split the piece to be blown up into smaller sections and then join them together. Another way of doing this would be to do the enlargement on a computer and print these out directly using a large format printer.

Whatever method you use, the final profile shape is then cut out of MDF with a band saw to create the former. Don't throw away the piece from which the former is cut out from – we will use this later on as a profile template. The former itself is now hot glued into its appropriate position on the MDF side profile to create a skeleton of the fuselage.

I now fill in the gaps between the formers with blocks of polyurethane foam – you can normally buy these from fibre-glass retailers. Polystyrene isn't good enough because it can't be smooth sanded, it easily breaks apart and will be attacked by polyester resin. This is also true of blue foam, so make sure that the foam you use has a fine grain and can take the resin that will be used later on. I tend to use polyester resin as the 'glue', as it's cheap and quick.

Once the whole body side has been covered in polyurethane blocks, I use a carving knife to get a rough shape by cutting down to just above the profile formers. I then use 80 grit sandpaper to sand the body to the shape of the formers. This isn't going to be the final shape so I don 't worry about dents, scratches and other surface imperfections at this point. The whole body is then sealed with polyester resin and allowed to dry overnight, which makes the body rigid and less prone to dents.

The next stage involves putting car body filler (make sure it is easily sandable) over the complete fuselage. Once dry, the body is then sanded to shape, using the profile template as a guide to the overall shape and size. I do not use electric sanders as I can't feel the shape as is being formed – I can if it is done by hand. It's a lot of work but for me the end result is so much better.

Above: Side view of the BO-105 cut out of MDF

Below: Formers added - notice the plastic kit of a BO-105 used to get the right former profile

Above: Blocks of polyurethane foam are glued in place between formers

Below: Foam blocks are cut down, covered with body filler and sanded to shape

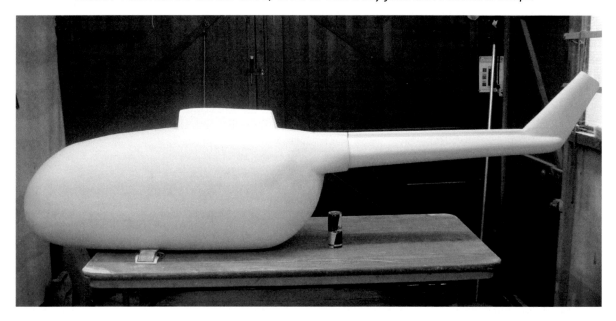

I now put on a primer–filler coat and sand this with 600-grade wet-and-dry paper to give a smooth finish. This shows up any imperfections such as pinholes and scratches that can be filled and then sanded down again.

Once complete I use a pencil to draw in the various panels, seam lines, doors and windows onto the body. A thin sticky-tape – something like Letraline from Letraset, is then placed over the pencil lines. I use .7mm width for window lines and 1mm width for panels.

To make sure these lines are in the right place I place the plug on a board with a marked out grid. I can use the grid lines to ensure that details such as windows and doors are in exactly the right place lengthways along the fuselage. To get them at the right height, I attach a length of wood to a set-square and make a pencil mark on the wood at the exact height where the panel lines need to be. Once I have done one side, I can then use the same mark to draw the line on the other side and at the right position on the board grid. This is particularly important for doors and undercarriage holes, as any misalignment will show up on the finished model.

The whole body is then sprayed again with a good coat of primer-filler. Once dry this filler is rubbed back with 800-grade wet-and-dry to the height of the thin-tape lines. The tape is then removed revealing recessed panel lines.

I now make any protruding panels out of thin ply, card or even adhesive vinyl and stick them into place. These are then hand painted with the same primer-filer and lightly sanded. The plug is now finished and is typically large and heavy. Having spent all this time on producing it, it's now about to be destroyed!

Making the Mould

Tail

As mentioned at the start of this chapter, because of the size of the Red Bull model I was making, I decided to keep the model in two parts – the main fuselage body and the tail - to make it easier to transport. However, even if you are building a one-piece model, it is still easier to make separate body and tail moulds, which will be split down the middle into two half's.

I start by making the tail mould first as when this is complete the tail section can be removed from the plug, which will make it easier to handle the main body when producing the remaining moulds.

The process starts by drawing a centre line down the length of the tail on both the top and bottom sides that indicate the two sides to be made. Onto this line I then place a 25 - 35mm tall piece of sealed MDF to act as shuttering, which is backed up with plasticine to hold it in place. Next I fit a former near the main body area, again supported by plasticine which defines the limit of the tail moulding. Male locating pegs are now fitted 15cm apart into the MDF along the length of the tail boom. This will allow the two half's of the mould to be lined up later on when making a complete tail boom.

I now polish the area to be made (I use Mirrorglaze No. 16 but you can also use PVA release agent), allow it to dry and then lightly buff the area. This process is then repeated a further five times so that a good layer of polish is built up. Once completely dry I brush onto the polished area a polyester gel coat, to which a red pigment has been added. The red colour will help later on when putting on the clear gel coat for the actual model parts. When dry, resin is used to bond tissue and 2-3 layers of matting onto the gel coat.

When cured the plasticine and shuttering are removed, but the half tail mould itself is left in place, complete with the flange that has been created by the matting. The flange and exposed tail area are now polished six times and female pegs are placed over the male pegs. This then has a gelcoat, tissue and matting as before.

When both sides of the tail mould have cured, holes are drilled through both sides so they can be clamped with nuts and bolts when making the tail itself. The two sides can now be taken off the plug and cleaned up. These moulds are now polished as before so that the two sides of the tail boom can be made. It is important that both sides are made at the same time.

I put paper into the mould to create a template of how much cloth will be required, which is then transferred to a cardboard template. This is then used to cut two layers of cloth for each side, making sure that the direction of the weave is different for each to give added strength to the part we're about to make.

Clear gel coat this time is applied to the moulds – having the mould in red will help you see that the coat is applied evenly. When dry I use epoxy resin to lay up the two layers of cloth on each mould and add carbon fibre to any area that needs strengthening such as the tail fin or where the tail meets the body. This is then placed into an oven at 35C to cure.

After 2-3 hours I take out the moulds to green-cut the excess cloth and then the two sides are bolted together along the length to ensure a tight fit. This is where the male and female locating pegs come in handy, as well as the aligned bolt-holes. A wet 20mm piece of tape is then put in place along the join line using a wooden rod to ensure it is in the right place. This is then left to cure overnight. In the morning you should have a completed tail.

The newly created tail is popped out of the mould and put back onto the main plug. This is done by cutting off the tail boom from the plug but ensuring that there is 70 - 90mm of the tail left on the body. Don't throw the cut-off tail plug away as it will come in useful later on.

The extra portion of the tail on the plug is now recessed with something like a Dremel grinding wheel so that the newly made tail fits snugly onto it, and that the surfaces of both plug and tail are level. I achieve this by applying a fillet of body filler onto the newly ground surface of the plug. I put Sellotape onto the inside and edge of the tail I've just made and then push the tail onto the plug. This should squeeze out any excess body filler, which can then be removed, leaving a tight fit. The Sellotape should ensure that the body filler does not adhere to the tail itself.

If you are making a model where the tail is to be permanently joined to the fuselage, I recommend that you do not join them until after fitting on some of the scale detail, which we will cover in chapter 12.

Windows

The next moulds to be made are the windows. This requires a four part process, which starts by making a female mould of each window. I do this by polishing the area of the window to be made, as with the tail mould.

Plasticine is then placed around the window area to be moulded, to stop the gel coat and fibreglass resin leaking out. It also gives the mould a defined edge. Gel coat is brushed into the mould area and when dry layup one layer of fibreglass matting. I only use one layer of matting because the resulting mould will only be used to create another mould, and then it is thrown away. The newly made mould is left overnight in a warm room to cure and, if the polish has done it's work, should come off quite easily.

The next step is to make a male mould from the female mould just made. This is done by polishing the inside of the female mould as before, applying gel coat and one layer of matting. Once cured, the new male mould can then be removed.

This needs to be turned into a solid object so that the vacuum forming process has something that won't give when the acetate material is pulled over it. I make this by placing the male mould, with the 'open' side facing down, on top of a piece of MDF that extends beyond the mould edge. The gaps that are left between the mould and the board are filled in with body-filler and sanded smooth.

This is now sealed with filler-primer and polished, along with the surrounding MDF board, followed by gel coat and one layer of matting. Make sure the matting extends to at least one inch onto the MDF board to create a lip. When cured, take off the newly created female mould.

The last step in creating the window mould is to create a solid male mould for the vacuum moulding process. This is done by polishing the inside of the mould and fixing it to a board so that lip is both at the top and absolutely level. I use a spirit level to achieve this.

High-temperature resin is now poured into the mould to fill it completely, scraping any excess resin from the top of the mould. This will ensure that the final window mould will sit flat when forming the windows.

The windows can now be formed using acetate sheet. I must admit that I get mine made by people who have the right equipment and expertise as I hate to see any imperfections caused by the moulding process. The acetate windows will have mould lines that indicate the extent of the window, but I leave an additional 5mm when cutting them so that they can be glued to the fuselage from the inside.

Panels and Doors

With the tail and window moulds finished, the next step is to make the various removable panels and doors. The process for doing this involves producing moulds for each individual item, actually making them from fiberglass and then fitting the completed item back onto the fuselage plug. To get the panels to fit snugly, the plug is recessed to accept them so that the overall contour of the body is kept smooth. This means that when the main body itself is made, I know the panels and doors will fit perfectly.

As with the windows, I surround the part to be made with plasticine. This is then polished as when making the other moulds. I now apply red gel coat and when set, I apply a layer of tissue followed by two layers of fibreglass matting with polyester resin.

After curing, the mould is taken off the plug, cleaned up and polished so that the finished item can be made. As with the tail I create a template of how much cloth will be required, which is then used to cut two layers of cloth making sure that the direction of the weave is different.

Clear gel coat is applied to the newly made mould, and when dry I use epoxy resin to lay up the two layers of cloth. This is then placed into an oven at 35C to cure. After 2-3 hours I take out the mould to green-cut the excess cloth back to the edge of the mould. It is then placed back into the oven for a further 9 hours.

I now go back to the main plug and cut out the part I've just made but leaving a 5mm lip on which the part can rest on. Having panel lines on the mould makes this an easier task. I now recess the lip on the main plug and apply a 10-15cm fillet of body filler onto the lip. I put Sellotape onto the part to be fitted to stop the body filler adhering to it and press it into place until the surface of the part and plug meet. Do not attempt to do the whole of the lip in one go - it's far easier to do this in smaller sections. The 'pressing' will squeeze out any excess body filler, which can then be removed.

Once this has been completed all around the lip, it can be lightly sanded and sealed with primer-filler paint. This process is repeated for the rest of the fuselage panels and doors.

Main Body

The main body mould is made in exactly the same way as the tail boom. MDF shuttering is fitted top and bottom down the length of the mould, backed up by plasticine. Male pegs

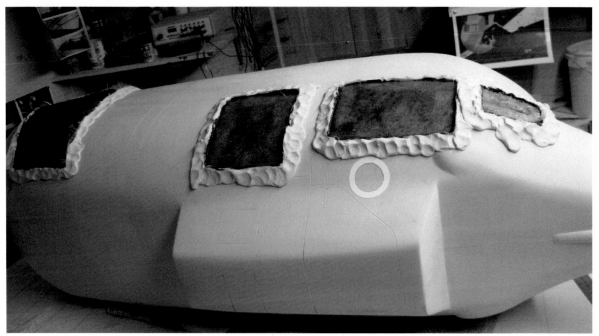

Above: Window mould created by placing plasticine around the area and applying cloth and resin

Below: Resulting window moulds ready for the acetate sheet.

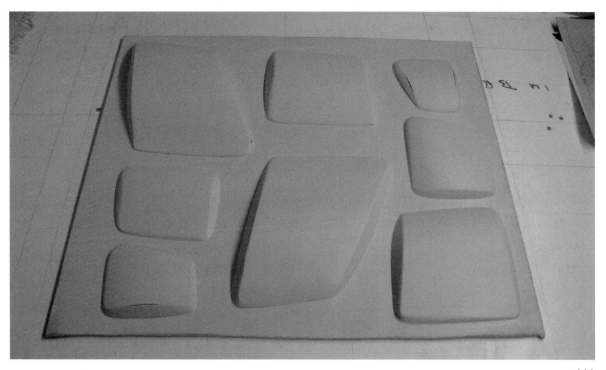

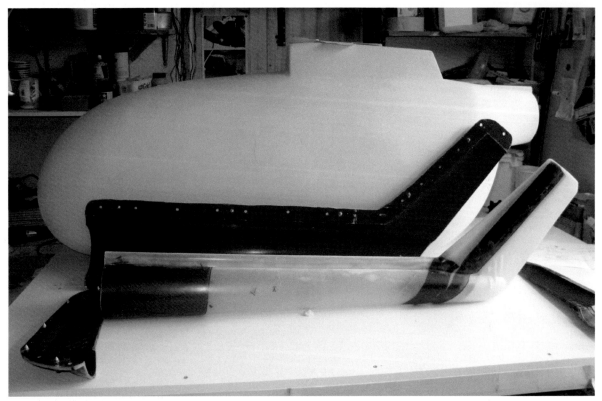

Above: Completed tail and tail mould - notice pegs on either side of the mould for aligning sides

Below: Main body mould - one side has been completed (in red), now making the second side

For more pictures of making the moulds, see the accompanying CD

are located down the length of the MDF, followed by polishing, gel coat, tissue and matting. When cured, the MDF can be removed, female pegs put in place along the newly created flange and the second side created.

Once the mould is ready I can make the actual fuselage, strengthening any weak or heavy load areas with carbon fibre as I did with the tail. Similarly, both halves are produced at the same time and joined together during the green cut stage.

At the end of all this work you should have a lightweight, accurate scale body, along with a set of moulds that can re-produce any part should they get damaged. Or you can produce another model. I did this with my Westland Scout. One model was for practice flights while the other had the full scale interior applied to it but was only flown at shows and competitions.

Fitting the Formers

The final step in completing the basic fuselage is to fit the formers that strengthen the model, for example alongside windows and door openings, and to which the undercarriage and mechanics are attached.

To make sure the profile is accurate, I use the plug from which the body was made and mark on the outside where the formers are to be located. I then use a saw to cut down the line of the formers, but only halfway down the side of the plug. Into these slots, pieces of card from old cornflakes packets are inserted, and a line drawn around where the card protrudes out of the fuselage. The card can then be taken out and trimmed to the line drawn, checking that it fits inside the actual fuselage.

This card is for one half of the fuselage. Reversing the card gives the other half of the fuselage, providing the body you have made is symmetrical. Once a snug fit is obtained, the card formers are then placed onto of a sheet of ply from which the real wooden formers can be cut out. These should now fit perfectly.

To get the right height for the rotor head, I place a few blocks of foam on the floor of the fuselage, and stand the mechanics on top so that the shaft is in the right position both vertically and horizontally. I have a good idea how big to make the blocks from the wallpaper drawing I used to make the MDF side profile.

Once I'm sure the mechanics are in the right place, I can now plan the woodwork that the mechanics will stand on. Once this is done I then permanently bond the formers to the fuselage. I do this by first tacking them into place with thick cyno and then reinforcing with fibreglass cloth and epoxy resin. One of the advantages of making the fuselage with clear gel coat is that you can see from the outside when the formers are in the right place. This process is repeated for all the formers in both the main body and the tail boom.

12. Completing the Body

This chapter assumes that we have a basic fuselage with formers in place that are drilled and ready to accept the mechanics. If you have bought a body kit, then hopefully reaching this stage should not take that much time. If you have a separate tail moulding as I did with my model, do not join it at this stage. It is far easier to do some of the early steps with the tail and body as separate items.

The following describes the order I used in detailing the Red Bull BO105 fuselage.

Preparing the fuselage

My first job is to prepare the fuselage. Whether you have built your own or bought a kit, the chances are that the fuselage will have some unsightly mould lines where the different parts of the fuselage have been joined together.

I scrape these off using a sharp knife, followed by 800 grit wet-and-dry paper. I also look out for any dents, scratches and pin-holes that need to be filled, which are then sanded back to a smooth finish.

I next clean up around any door areas making sure that the door lip isn't too large and has a consistent width around it. There is nothing worse than seeing a beautifully crafted door, which when opened shows a totally non-scale surround.

Removable panels, exhaust ports, air intakes and other holes are now carefully cut out. I like to leave the main windows until later to avoid breaking or stressing the window bars that would remain.

Undercarriage and footsteps

At this stage we need to decide on whether the undercarriage is to be removable or permanently fixed in place. With the BO105, I made it removable as this makes painting a lot easier. If your subject is all one colour - for example on a military machine, then having a fixed undercarriage is not so much of a problem.

For the BO105 I made left and right hand carriages that plugged into a tube within the fuselage. Fitting the undercarriage at this stage provides a stable platform on which to add further scale detailing.

On most undercarriages there will be some kind of footboard or step. I make the footboards out of plywood or hardwood, which are sealed and sanded to a smooth finish. I then roughen up the area where the step is by mixing sand with the paint that will be used. You can also buy non-slip materials from most model shops.

If there are steps leading into the cabin, I make these from thin aluminum sheet. This is where empty drink cans come in very useful.

Flooring

The next step to is to create the floor inside the cockpit. I start this by working out where I'm going to place the radio, gyro and any servos required for things such as moveable joysticks, foot-pedals and moving searchlights. Fortunately with today's equipment being small and light, it's possible to hide these components away, which for me is under the floor area.

In order to get access, I make my floors in sections that are held in place by strong magnets. By doing it this way you can arrange that for large sections of the interior to be removed as a complete unit. For example, one front seat and its immediate floor area can all be moved in one go. Not only does this give access to the radio under the floor, but it also makes building the seat much easier as it can be done outside of the model itself.

This does mean that when I plan the floor I'm mindful of what can be built onto a floor section and whether or not I'll be able to take the completed unit out of the door when finished.

The BO105 has large rear doors that makes the creation of the interior fairly easy. With this in mind I decided to have six floor compartments. To hold the floor in place I put in a number of cross members so that each compartment floor is supported on all four sides. I then glue powerful magnets into the corner of each compartment and embed a thin strip of metal from a baked bean can into the floor itself. I find that the best magnets for this kind of work have to be bought from specialist suppliers. Unfortunately, most magnets you get from shops are often too big and not powerful enough for our needs.

For the floor itself, you can buy plasti-card sheets that resemble a non-slip metal floor, but for my models these are usually not big enough. I therefore make my own by gluing three of these sheets together and polishing them six times to make a mould (see chapter 11). I then lay onto this mould thin carbon fibre-cloth with resin, followed by a sheet of 2mm ply. On top of this I place a large board with weights so that it presses together the fibre/ply/resin sandwich. The result is a strong, very light scale floor that can be cut to size as required.

Doors and door hinges

My next job is to tackle the doors. I make mine so that the handles actually work and operate a rod mechanism that locks into both the top and bottom of fuselage. I use thin brass sheet silver soldered to a small brass tube for the handle. This tube then passes through the door to which another small plate is silver soldered, which will be attached to a rod. It's a bit fiddly but well worth it when you see the result. I've also been known to add a small, powerful magnet to make sure they stay closed in flight.

I also make my own door hinges from brass sheet as I find most commercial hinges far too big to give a true scale appearance.

As well as having two 'normal' doors, the BO105 has two large rear sliding doors that give access to the cabin and one huge cargo door at the rear. I spent many hours working out how to achieve this but was very pleased with the result.

Panels, louvers and air-intakes

Once the doors are finished, I move onto fitting air intakes, vents and non-functioning exhaust pipes. Again I tend to find that these items can be pretty grotesque in some commercial kits so I would recommend making your own. They are typically not hard to do and involves in making up a plug out of body filler and then creating your own mould. I know it takes time, but you will be so much happier with the end result.

With louvers, I make mine from thin aluminum or litho plate if I can get hold of it. I mark out the vent lines on the plate and drill a small hole at either end of the lines. I then carefully cut between the holes and lift up one side of the cut. On the BO105 model it took a couple of goes to get it right, but again I'm very pleased with the end result.

Tailboom and fins

The next task for me is to fit the tail boom to the main body. If this is to be removable then it means installing a coupling that enables the tail drive to easily connect simply by pushing the two sides together. It also means installing internal flanges so that the tail can be bolted together inside of the main body. This will require internal access to the bolts but arranged in a way that they cannot be seen from the outside. I do this by making a panel on the body near the coupling to be removable so that I can get access to the bolts with a suitable driver.

The tail should now be fitted. If this is to be permanently, then we don't need to be worried about the tail drive at this moment.

I now install a bar through the tail onto which I can place the stabiliser fins. Even if I have a fixed tail, I still make the fins removable as these are then less likely to get damaged when transporting the model. When drilling the hole through the tail, do ensure that it is exactly at 90 degrees to the main shaft. I use a 5mm carbon rod or stainless steel bar onto which the fin unit can slide.

Above: Completed bodyshell - notice carbon fibre to strengthen weak areas

Below: Installing the floor - the mechanics and turbine are in place to ensure everything fits

Above: Doors and grills in place ready for final painting
Below: Rear working doors - hinges and door catches made from thin sheet brass

Wiring looms

On my model I wanted to have the lighting replicate the exact sequence of lights of the full size Red Bull machine. When I saw the full size version I made a note of what lights flashed and when. Back at home I contacted a friend who can supply the right colour lights and the exact sequence I required. This isn't cheap - but there again radio control helicopters is not necessarily a cheap hobby. The total cost was around £70, which I thought was worthwhile. The lights are tiny but as they used high visibility LED's, the effect is amazing and can be seen even in bright daylight.

I fit in the wiring by using adhesive cable ties to keep the wires in place and where they cannot be accidentally cut. I put plugs on those lights going to the tail fins so that the fins can be easily removed. I also make up wiring looms for any remote servos and again make sure that the wiring is clearly labelled and neatly installed. Where I have working features such as moving joysticks, flashing lights, etc. I install a separate battery and in some models these are operated by a second receiver so I can keep my main receiver and batteries dedicated to flying the model.

I arrange for all switches and charging plugs to be mounted on a strong panel that is usually hidden behind a removable grill. By doing this there are no loose leads to get in the way, and starting the model is a simple, straight-forward affair.

Tail rotor, nuts and bolts

I now refit the mechanics and install a flexi-drive tail rotor drive system, the tail rotor gearbox and push rod. I try and use a tail rotor gearbox that is quite near to scale, which some of the specialist vendors such as Heli-Factory can supply. Otherwise I will cyno small bits of wood or use body filler to turn the gearbox into something that resembles the full size. Once I've checked that these are all working fine, I remove just the mechanics and tail gearbox, leaving the rest in place.

My next step is to add any small nuts, bolts, screws etc. that can be seen on the body of the full size machine. It is often this minute detail that makes the difference between a model and a miniature replica. To do this well I use real miniature nuts and bolts as they look sharp and add realism. They are expensive but in my mind are worth it. Although most model shops do not stock this size you can often get them from enthusiast shops that sell miniature replica trains and boats, as well as at model engineering shows.

Fire extinguisher systems

It's worth commenting at this point on the subject of fire. Soon after finishing the BO105, complete with all its scale details and fantastic paint job, I took it out for its maiden test flight. I started the turbine in the usual way and was waiting for the rotor blades to spin up when I noticed traces of smoke coming from the cabin. As I started to shut down the engine down there was a 'woomph' noise followed by flames coming out of the exhaust pipes, doors, panels …. It was well and truly alight.

I always have a fire extinguisher to hand but the amount of damage the fire did in those few seconds was incredible and it took me another year to repair the damage, in fact far longer than in building the model to begin with. It appears that the turbine had 'coughed' and set light to the internal propane gas–line, which then took on the role of a flame thrower inside the confines of the fuselage.

You are never too old to learn and now when I construct a model I build in special fire extinguisher tubes that should a fire break out again, will immediately put out the flames. This may sound like overkill, but when you have invested 5 or 600 hours of time in a world-class model, it's heart breaking to see it destroyed by something that was preventable in the first place.

Spot lights

I love to build spotlights that are held within the body of the fuselage, but on command will swivel down and come on. These add a certain 'wow' factor and are surprisingly easy to do.

In making these I first find a cardboard roll that is the right diameter for the body. For a large search-light this may be a toilet-paper roll, while for a small light this may be the tube from a baking foil roll. The cardboard roll is then stiffened by soaking it in cyno. Mirrorlight ply is then wrapped around the outside to form the tube which can then be cut to the right length..

I use balsa wood to make the front surround and back of the tube, and the reflector and bulb from a torch to make the light. For a really bright light I use 6-volt halogen lamps made for flush- mounted ceiling lights. These come with an integral reflector so I only have to make up a cable to attach to the bulb.

For the bracket holding the lamp, I make a solid former and then laminate layers of mirrorlight ply in a U-shape until the thickness I want is built up. This produces a very strong, yet light bracket. I also do the same with the mounting bracket that is fitted to the fuselage floor. I then add rivets, tiny nuts and bolts, and copper wires to mimic the detail of the full size unit. This is then mounted into the fuselage where servos can move the light left, right, up down, as well as turning the light on and off.

Aerials

I make my own aerials from small pieces of plastic or wire cut to length. On larger aerials such as those found in military machines I may make up the aerial frame from plywood or fiberglass from a mould. For smaller aerials, the base is simply a blob of body filler that is carved to shape.

Above and right: Different views in making a working, movable spotlight - from Len's London fire brigade BK117.

Above: Dummy exhaust pipes

Left: Clamps with miniature nuts and bolts add to realism on the undercarriage.

Above: Painting in progress with my Kiowa standing guard   Below: Job done

Whatever size of aerial, a bolt or length of threaded rod is then bonded into the aerial base so that it protrudes from the bottom. This then fits through a hole in the fuselage where it can be firmly bolted into place. Making them removable means I can paint them and the main body separately, which greatly simplifies the areas that need to be masked.

Degreasing

Now that most of the external work has been done, I like to thoroughly de-grease the whole model. It's vital to get rid of any polish that may have been left from the moulding process, as well as any sweat and dirt that can come from your hands as part of every day life. The smallest trace - even if you can't see or feel it, can ruin any paintwork that is applied later on.

You can do this either by using a commercial body wash available from paint shops or by washing the fuselage with hot water that has a mixture of washing-up liquid and vinegar. I use a clean cloth to get into all creases and mould lines to make sure I get into every area. Next I rub down the complete fuselage using 800-1200 grit wet-and-dry paper. The fuselage is then washed down with clean water and left to dry. As there is still some work to be done on the fuselage, it is important to keep the body as clean as possible and to constantly wipe areas where you have worked on. Keeping your hands clean on any subsequent operations will help.

The body is now ready for an undercoat - I use a good quality 2-part undercoat which normally only requires a single coat.

Rivet detail

I am now at the stage where I like to put on the rivet detail. Again I find the rivets that can be bought commercially are far too big for our purposes. What I do is to first draw some pencil lines which indicate the rivet lines. To make sure these lines are the same height and spacing on each side I use the same setup with a set-square and a length of wood as I did when drawing the panel lines on the plug as described in chapter 11.

I then put on the 'rivets' by applying PVA glue that is dispensed from a syringe. I use different size needles to match the different kinds of rivets you find on the full size. In order to have a constant flow of glue, I arrange elastic bands around the plunger of the syringe so that there is steady pressure. All I have to do then is work along the line and dabbing the needle onto it at regular intervals. Once the glue has dried, I lightly rub down the rivets with dry 1000 – 1200 grit wet-and-dry paper to take off any peaks that may have formed.

Windows

My final step in this whole process is to cut out the windows. This is a relatively straightforward job and so I don't have much to say on it. The exterior detail work is now complete and ready to have scale details added to the inside of the fuselage. However, my preference at this stage is to paint the body.

Painting

As mentioned above, the model should have already been rubbed down, degreased and had a good undercoat applied. If the model is to have multiple colours such as the case with the Red Bull machine, I always put on the lightest colour first. In my case this was white and so I sprayed the whole machine white. I do this by first applying a light or dust coat, wait 10-15 minutes until tacky and then put on a wet coat. This is left to dry overnight.

When it is dry I mask up where the next lighter colour is to go – for the Red Bull this was red. I make sure that all the areas I want to stay white are completely covered. The next colour is then sprayed on. I repeat the masking and spraying process for the next lightest colour and so on until all the colours have been applied.

When all the paint has dried I then spray on a clear laquer coat. If you are like me and don't want to feel the edges between the different colours then you should put on the clear laquer coat on top of each colour as you do them. Then the edges should be treated to a 1200 grit wet-and-dry rub making sure that you don't break through the laquer coat.

Graphics

On the Red Bull BO105, there are a number of graphics including lettering and a small cartoon character. The cartoon was far to small to mask up and spray so what I did was to enlarge the photo I had taken of it to the actual size I wanted for the model. It was then printed out onto the best quality photo paper and cut out by hand. I then carefully scrape the back of the photo to remove as much of the paper as I dare. Damping down the back of the photo can help with the paper removal. When I first used this technique I would often ruin two or three photos before I had one that was OK. I must admit I tend to get it right first time these days.

The resulting image is then attached to the fuselage by applying a solid adhesive such as Prit-Stick to the back of the photo. This is then laquered to protect it. On some intricate large designs you can also create a photoshop image and have this sent away to a company who can then make a mask from it, which makes the masking up a lot easier.

With miniature writing I enlarge a photo of the area six or seven times larger than I want. I have a friend who then turns this into a Letraset image at the right size, which can then be rubbed onto the finished model and laquer applied.

Once all the graphics and paintwork has been completed, I put on one or two final clear coats of laquer.

13. Interior Scale Detail

The difference between a good model and a scale model in my mind is all down to the interior. It's fairy easy to make a model that replicates the external appearance of a full size machine but the builders expertise is only shown when the inside is as good as the real thing. Two things conspire against the builder - the lack of space due to the necessary placement of mechanics, engine and radio systems, and the cramped nature of that space which makes it very difficult to work on.

Many commercial fuselages only allow for the very front of the cabin to have any scale detail and quite often the scale interiors they provide are not very good. For this reason I build my own fuselages, which tend to be on the large size. However, if you do have a commercial fuselage you can still make a great job of the interior – but it will usually mean throwing away what was provided and starting afresh.

To make building the interior easier I do not fit the windows or doors, and much of the detail is made attached to removable floor panels, so it can be built outside of the fuselage. If you are going to do this then do make sure the finished item can pass through an open door if you want to get it out again when the model is complete.

Seats

To make the seats I use a 'side-on' photo of the full size. This is then enlarged to the size I want for the model. This side view then allows you to easily create a side template of the seat. We need to make two of these – one for each side.

To get the width of each seat you need either a 'front-on' picture of the full size, which is probably impractical given the cramped nature of most cockpits, or you can work it out from a plan view of the full size and seeing where each seat starts an ends. Another method I sometimes employ is to make up the seats from the plastic kit from which I made the fuselage formers. These completed items can then be measured and the width of the seat deduced.

The basic frame of the seat can now be made – I use ply for the sides of each seat and either foam or balsa sheet to fill in the seat between the two sides. This is then carved and sanded to shape. Once I'm happy with the basic seat I then turn it into a mould as covered in chapter 11. If you don't want to do this then you can use the seat just made as a former to produce another one.

To this basic seat I then add small details such as map pockets, bolts and anything else that protrudes and can be seen on the photos. This is then painted. The next step is to then work out the mounting of the seat. On the BO105 the seats are adjustable back and forward, so I made up a rack that copies the full size machine. On my Westland Scout I made the seat so that it also went up and down which is worth more points in a competition.

For the seat cushions, finding the right material can take a long time. I take a photo of the material and scour second hand shops, looking at old clothes. With the BO105 I found a shirt that was the right colour and had the right weave but it didn't have any red dots. So I put these on with a fine-line marker pen.

The material is then applied to foam and made into cushions of the right size. Despite what others may think, my wife Olive doesn't do this job – she is more at home with fibre-glassing a mould so it's me who has the expertise with needle and thread.

The last step is to make up the seat belts. You can buy commercial kits that will save you a lot of time, or you can make all the buckles and adjusters from thick plastic sheet. On my BO105 I made the seat belts adjustable and on some models they also fasten with a satisfying 'clunk-click'. On my N4 Dauphin the seat belt even reeled back on their own tensioners!

Dashboards

Most commercial kits I've seen have very poor dashboards, so again I would recommend that you make your own. The first task is to make a cardboard template of the facia onto which dials and switches will be mounted. You can get the size of this from a plastic kit, which is then scaled up to the size you need.

The next task is to build the consol onto which the facia will sit. I usually make mine either out of a combination plywood and balsa wood, or from a block of foam. The important thing to remember is that the facia must be able to fit into a recess. The consol is then sanded to shape. Now we can add any extra 'lumps and bumps' as well as any nuts and bolts seen on the full size. This detail will really show up on the finished model and adds to the realism. The consol body is then painted.

To make the facia detail I first machine the bezels that surround each dial out of brass or aluminium tube that is the right size. I use a lathe to carefully cut very thin slices – this is something that needs a lot of patience if the rings are to maintain their shape while cutting.

I now cut the facia itself out of plasti-card using the cardboard template I made earlier. I enlarge a photo of the full-size facia to the right size for the model and use this to locate where the bezels fit onto the facia panel. Where these bezels are mounted onto a smaller panel, I cut these out and then secure both the smaller panels and bezel rings in place with a dab of cyno.

The switches are made from panel pins and tiny washers that mimic the back plate of the switch. These are again put in place using cyno. I then add in all the rivets, screws and whatever else is in the picture onto the facia panel.

The facia can then be undercoated and sprayed to the colour of full-size machine.

We now need to decide if the instruments are to have lights.

If the panel is to **have lights** then the facia is mounted onto a thick clear sheet of acetate and the centres cut out of each bezel that is to be lit up. Behind each cut-out a card is made which has a photo of the right dial on it. This is then stuck into place but trapping a small light in the gap. The Wires from each light should then be made into a wiring loom and a suitable plug attached. The facia can then be backed with a further sheet of plastic to protect the wiring.

If the panel is to have **no lights** then I print out high quality photos of each dial at the right size for the model. These are cut out and stuck in place within the bezel using a solid glue stick such as Prit-stick. When dry the bezels can be filled with three or four coats of household clear varnish, making sure each layer is dry before applying the next. This gives a concave glass effect on each bezel, which when viewed from the side (the view the judges will see), looks perfect.

I then use restorers frame rubbing compound and weathering powders on the bezels and switches that makes them look used. The completed unit can now be screwed in its recess in the consol. Again I mount my consol's on a removable floor panel that is held in place by strong magnets.

The above procedure is replicated for the centre consol.

Control columns and pedals

I like to make the joysticks on my models so they can move left, right, back and forward. The easiest way to achieve this is to have a bolt that protrudes from the base of the stick, which goes into a standard ball joint that is firmly attached to the floor.

The ball in the ball link is drilled out to accept the bolt, which is then bolted into place with the remainder of the bolt having a clevis that is used as a lever actuated by two servos and two ball links.

The joystick itself is made up from bent wire/tube with body filler used to mould the grip and floor parts. If the joystick is movable, then I make gaiters by coating a former that has been sealed, with six coats of liquid rubber. When dry this can then be peeled off the former and stuck onto a template at the base of the stick with silicon sealant.

The same technique can be applied to pedals.

I operate the joystick and pedals from a second receiver and battery that can be turned off in flight. The servos to the pedals and joystick are wired so that they move at the same time as the pitch control of the main rotor blades.

Fire Extinguishers

It's the little details that really make the difference, particularly if they work. One such item is a fire extinguisher that actually sprays water. I make these by inserting an eyedropper rubber into a metal tube that is of the right diameter of the extinguisher being made. The top of the extinguisher is shaped from balsa/body filler with a thin tube passing through it and attaching to the eyedropper. This unit is then painted to the right colours and any appropriate lettering added. The base of the tube is left open so that I can press the rubber inside to deflate it, it is then loaded by holding the thin tube in water and releasing the rubber.

When I show the extinguisher to the judges, I push my finger in the base of the canister and squirt them, which always looks impressive.

Pilot

Every scale model that flies needs a pilot. Over the years the best approach I've found is to visit a large toyshop and go through all the 'action-men' figures to get one that is the closest to the size you need. I then modify it to meet my needs, which typically involves shortening or enlarging limbs, as well as making them bend more easily so that they fit the controls.

On some of my models I've inserted servos so that the pilot can wave and move their head – I did warn you that I'm quite obsessed when it comes to scale detail.

Maps and other details

As most seats and doors have some form of pocket, you want something to go into them. Maps are quite appropriate and are very easy to do. I like to download a map from the Internet of the place where the competition is to be held. I then print this out and carefully fold it up, but making sure the judges can see that it is of the current location.

For the Red Bull BO105, I made miniature Red Bull drink cans. These were turned to the right size from a suitable diameter tube, and a groove made at the top and bottom to simulate the can top, using a lathe. I then got hold of a full size can, drank the contents, took off the top and bottom and split the can down one side and laid it flat. I took a photo of the outside label and printed it out to the right size for the can I had just made. The photo was then cut out and glued to the can - the result is a perfect replica!

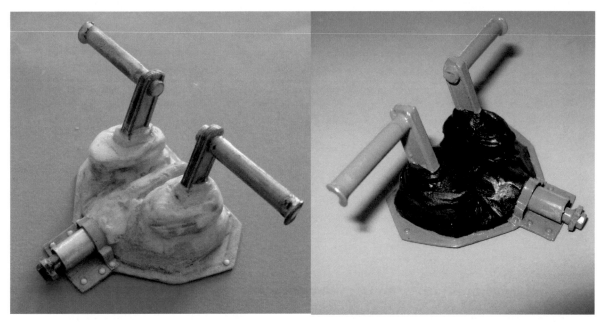

Above: Footpedals made from wood, metal tube and body filler - but the finished item looks great

Below: Under floor servo arrangement to operate joysticks or control columns

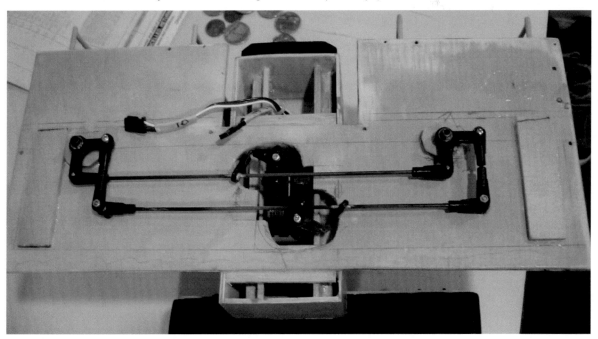

Above: Making the frames for the seats and cockpit of a Bell Huey

Right and Below: The finished items in place

14. Preparing for Competition

If you have spent many, many hours in building a great looking, accurate model, the last thing you want to do is fail on the simple, minor points. I made that mistake the first time I attended the prestigious Top Gun event in the US. I forgot some of the documentation, which lost me a lot of points and ultimately the competition as I missed out on first place by two tenths of a point.

Here are the things that I think are important and can make the difference between winning and coming second.

Documentation

In most national competitions, competitors are required to submit documentation of the full size machine they have modelled. Even if they don't, or if all the judges need are a few photographs, I would still recommend that you produce an extensive set of documents including a 3-view drawing, paint chips, and photos of the subject that show off your model from the best possible angles. These photos must come from the original and not your model.

The judges will typically have a judging sheet that they will use to go through the model in a particular order – e.g. undercarriage, rotor head, tail rotor, interior cabin, etc. You can usually find out this order in advance of the competition. I then use this order to assemble my documentation into a nice, smart binder, as this will make the judges life (and yours) so much easier. If there is more than one judge, I will assemble multiple copies of the documentation so that each judge has their own copy.

Flying schedule

With most scale competitions, there will be a session when the model is to be flown in a scale like manner. This means not flying it too fast, performing manoeuvres that the full-size would never do, or turning and changing height far too quickly. However, that doesn't mean that the flight should be boring either.

I've been to a lot of scale competitions where the flights have been dull and unimaginative. Where the pilots have kept the models within 20 metres of where they are standing and the only thing they have tackled is flying in a circle.

There is nothing more impressive than a scale model being flown in an impressive way. For me that includes using up the whole of the flight line, and taking the model 300 metres or so away. When I do a low pass, it's really low and for added effect I can make it fast. It's all scale but it has the 'wow' factor. So when planning your schedule make it scale but make it impressive. Just go for it – which brings me to my next point ….

Practice

Practice, practice and even more practice – there is no substitute for stick time. Even though I have been flying for over 40 years I still practice. But what may surprise you is that I practice the basic maneuvers – hovering, scale take off's, landing and so on. I'm still amazed at good, experienced modellers who can't hover on a marked out spot. Sure they can hover – at various heights and in various places, but the mark of a good flier is to hover at an exact height at an exact point and not wander from it.

And I practice in all weather conditions – wind, sun, cold, and sometimes rain. Practice will pay off. There have been some competitions where I have been the only pilot who was willing to fly because of the conditions. If you are competing with pilots who only fly when it is sunny and calm you will be at a distinct advantage if the conditions are anything else. Practicing in bad conditions also helps you to get to know your model and gives you so much more confidence that tackling the harder maneuvers isn't the problem that most people think it is. If you are one of these people who do not want to risk their model, then build a second one of the same weight but with less detail to practice on.

Improving the model

You never really finish building a scale model helicopter – there's always room for improvement. As I have previously mentioned, I like to continually improve mine. I originally spent around 350 hours building my military Westland Scout, which was good enough to win the US National Championship in 2006. For 2007 I improved the scale detail by redoing much of the exterior – adding pipes and additional nuts and bolts I had left off. I also changed a few details that on further examination with the photographs of the original, were wrong. It won that year as well.

For 2008 I wanted to add something special so I spent a another 120 hours on adding rockets. Although these do not necessarily gain me more points, the finished machine when flying looks so more impressive. It won again. By 2009, I had now spent around 800 hours in total, and it won for a fourth time. I could have gone on improving it but had decided that I wanted a new challenge – which is where the Red Bull BO105 came in. As it turned out it wasn't finished in time and so I didn't return to defend my title. Which brings me to my last and the most important point ...

Just enjoy it!

It may surprise you but the main reason why I build high quality models isn't just to win competitions. It's primarily so that other people can look at them and go 'wow', and secondarily so that I can look at it and know that I've done a good job. If the result is good enough to win a competition then that's the 'icing on the cake'. One of the reasons for doing the Red Bull BO105 was so that I could fly an aerobatic schedule in a scale helicopter competition, that was still in-keeping with the original. Now that's what I call fun and 'a bit of a challenge'!

Appendix: Major Championships

The following is a list of results from some of the major championships (well those I can remember) I have entered over the past 35 years.

Year	Event	Location	Category	Place
1977	British Nationals	England	F3C	1st place
1977	British Nationals	England	Scale	1st place
1978	British Nationals	England	F3C	1st place
1979	British Nationals	England	F3C	1st place
1980	British Nationals	England	F3C	1st place
1981	BRCHA	Woburn, England	Novelty	1st place
1981	BRCHA	Woburn, England	Scale	1st place
1981	BRCHA	Woburn, England	F3C	1st place
1981	Pontins	England	Scale	1st place
1981	Eurocup	Vilvoorde, Holland	F3C	3rd place
1981	Slough fly in scale	England	Scale	1st place
1981	Woburn Abbey expert	England	Scale	1st place
1982	International Meeting	Nancy, France	F3C	1st place
1982	Pontins	England	Scale	1st place
1983	Jupiter Club	Vinlo, Holland	Scale	1st place
1983	Slough Scale fly in	England	Scale	2nd place
1983	Cambridge FAI	Norwich, England	F3C	2nd place
1983	Tign Valley model fly-in	Norwich, England	F3C	1st place
1983	Slough Helicpters FAI	England	F3C	1st place
1983	Eynesford	England	Scale	2nd place
1983	Salemac	England	F3C	2nd place
1983	Woburn Abbey	England	Scale	1st place
1983	Slough fly in scale	Slough, England	Scale	1st place

Major championships cont'd

Year	Event	Location	Category	Place
1983	Bombay air spectacular	India	Best in show	1st place
1983	Schluter cup	Germany		4th place
1983	Eurocup	England	F3C	4th place
1984	Fesitval Costa Del Sol,	Spain	Scale	1st place
1984	Slough Scale fly in	England	Scale	1st place
1984	Norwich fly-in	England	FAI	1st place
1984	Norwich fly-in	England	Best in show	1st place
1984	Norwich fly-in	England	Scale	1st place
1984	Slough Scale fly in	England	Scale	1st place
1984	Woburn Cup	Woburn	F3C	1st place
1984	British Nationals	England	F3C	1st place
1984	Schluter cup	Germany		4th place
1984	Ermelo	Holland	Scale	1st place
1984	British Nationals	England	Scale	1st place
1985	US Nationals	USA	Scale	2nd place
1985	US Nationals	USA	F3C	4th place
1985	ROMEO USA	USA	Novelty	1st place
1985	Mid-America greatest helicopter fun fly	USA	Novelty	1st place
1985	Scottish heli nationals	Scotland	F3C	1st place
1985	Schluter cup	Germany		3rd place
1985	British Nationals	England	F3C	1st place
1986	German sports masters	Germany	Scale	2nd Place
1986	Sandown park	England	Scale	1st place
1986	Scottish heli nationals	Scotland	F3C	1st place
1986	Schluter cup	Germany		3rd place
1986	Sandown park	England	Scale	1st place

Major championships cont'd

Year	Event	Location	Category	Place
1986	Someren	Belgium	Scale	1st place
1986	Balgnac	France	F3C	2nd pace
1987	Schluter cup	Germany		6th place
1987	Badmac Heli	England	Novelty 1&2	1st place
1987	Badmac Heli	England	Scale	1st place
1987	Robbe Scale masters	POKAL, Germany	Scale	1st place
1988	Retford scale	Norwich, England	Scale	1st place
1988	BEHC Concourse de elegance	England	Scale	1st place
1988	British Nationals	England	Scale	1st place
1988	British Nationals	England	F3C	1st place
1988	Bath helicopter club	England	Six categories	1st place
1989	Max Coote memorial helicopter trophy	England	F3C	1st place
1989	Schluter cup	Germany		4th place
1990	BRCHA	England	F3C	1st place
1990	Scottish heli nationals	Scotland	F3C	1st place
1990	Scottish heli nationals	Scotland	Scale	1st place
1990	British Nationals	England	F3C	1st place
1990	Clareville	USA	F3C	1st place
1990	Woburn	Woburn, England	F3C	1st place
1990	Schluter cup	Germany		3rd place
1990	Ulster Nationals	N. Ireland	Novelty	1st place
1990	Max Coote memorial helicopter trophy	England	F3C	1st place
1991	Ulster Nationals	N. Ireland	F3C	1st place
1991	Ulster Nationals	N. Ireland	Scale	1st place

Major championships cont'd

Year	Event	Location	Category	Place
1991	Schluter cup	Germany		2nd place
1991	New Zealand National championships	New Zealand	F3C	1st place
1991	Scottish Nationals	Scotland	F3C	1st place
1992	Campo de Gibralter	Gibralter	Novelty	1st place
1992	Schluter cup	Germany		4th place
1993	Ulster Nationals	N. Ireland	F3C	1st place
1994	Schluter cup	Germany		1st place
1994	Schluter cup	Holland		1st place
1995	Schluter cup	Germany		6th place
1995	Schluter cup	Holland		1st place
1996	European Hirobo Cup		F3C	4th place
1996	European championships		F3C	4th place
1999	Marzo	Malaga Spain	Scale	Best in show
2001	Heli Heatwave	Fort Worth Texas, USA	Outstanding Contribution award	
2001	Top Gun	Miami USA	Scale	2nd place
2001	Top Gun	Miami USA	Scale	Best cockpit interior
2002	Circumgyration	San Francisco	Life time achievement award for outstanding contriibution to helicopter modelling	
2002	Eynesford scale fly in	England	Scale	1st place
2003	Circumgyration	San Francisco, USA	Scale	Best in show
2004	Stanford Top Fun	USA	Novelty	1st place
2006	US Nationals	USA	Scale	1st place
2007	US Nationals	USA	Scale	1st place
2008	US Nationals	USA	Scale	1st place
2009	US Nationals	USA	Scale	1st place

Index